WHAT PEOPLE ARE SAYING ABOUT *STRONG ENOUGH TO LAST*

"David Boyd masterfully captures insights related to training and discipling children. Through his decades of involvement in children's ministry he has seen what works and what doesn't. *Strong Enough to Last* will give every teacher and leader the perspectives they need to fulfill their calling to 'make disciples.'"
—*Rod Loy, senior pastor, First Assembly of God, North Little Rock, Arkansas*

"Leaders often wonder if they're making a difference. In *Strong Enough to Last*, David Boyd provides insights that help leaders focus on the most important outcomes to build a strong faith foundation in the children within their ministry. His personal experiences growing up as a bus-kid, time in the local church, and years leading a national children's ministry movement provide the expertise that assures readers they can trust the wisdom captured on these pages."
—*Mark Entzminger, senior director of children's ministries, General Council of the Assemblies of God, Springfield, MO*

"I have watched David Boyd, and his wife, Mary, reach and disciple children for over three decades. This book captures David's heart for discipleship in a very real and practical manner. David weaves his own testimony from age twelve on throughout the text. Kid-tested discipleship examples from his life and others are seamlessly provided alongside practical how-to directives. His blueprint for discipleship will soon be adapted by the many who read this book. I fully recommend this book for any KidMin leader with a heart to see kids fully engaged in the Christian life."
—*Dick Gruber, DMin, professor of children and family studies, University of Valley Forge, Phoenixville, PA*

"I have known David Boyd and worked alongside him, for many years. When it comes to impacting children and youth, I don't think he has an equal. His leadership over the Assemblies of God "Boys and Girls Missions Challenge" has resulted in tens of millions of dollars raised to reach kids around the world for Christ. This book is going to help many, many people to direct kids to Jesus. I'm excited about endorsing it! I think you will be excited (and fulfilled) in reading it!"
—*Dan Betzer, pastor, First Assembly of God, Ft. Myers, FL; general presbyter of the General Council of the Assemblies of God*

"Wow! As both a children's pastor and a parent, I found this book to be incredibly challenging and thought provoking. It is absolutely full of practical ideas that I can apply today to the spiritual development of my children."
—*Kelly Presson, children's pastor, Christian Celebration Center, Midland, MI*

"David Boyd is not only a master storyteller, he's a passionate communicator who can't help but fire up the reader. I have admired David's leadership for a long time. He's a pioneer in Kidmin and has influenced countless kids pastors and leaders to pursue God's calling on their lives to reach the children of our world. In *Strong Enough to Last*, David shares his personal experiences and wisdom to help every church and Kidmin leader make a lasting impact in their community and the world!"
—*Brian Dollar, associate and kids pastor at First Assembly of God, North Little Rock, AK; creator of High Voltage Kids Ministry; author of I Blew It and Talk Now and Later*

"This book is a must read for anyone in children's ministry. *Strong Enough to Last* comes out of David's heart and life because for years he's lived and modeled these eight fundamentals. It's an honor for me to recommend this book for children's ministers regardless of their age or experience."
—*Jim Wideman, children's ministry pioneer, author, and leadership coach*

"*Strong Enough to Last* is an outstanding book that every pastor, associate, and children and youth minister should read. It's a strategic resource for building a strong foundation for the next generation. It's time we recognize that the greatest commodity of any nation is its next generation. This book is a wakeup call to us in the body of Christ that it's time to build within our children and youth 'A faith that is strong enough to keep them anchored in Christ.'"
—*Rod Baker, director of Victory Missions, Tulsa, OK*

STRONG ENOUGH TO LAST

BUILDING SPIRITUAL DEPTH INTO OUR KIDS

DAVID J. BOYD

Gospel Publishing House

Published by Gospel Publishing House
1445 N. Boonville Ave.
Springfield, Missouri 65802
www.myhealthychurch.com

Cover design and interior design and formatting by Prodigy Pixel (www.prodigypixel.com)

02-4222

ISBN: 978-1-60731-469-1

Printed in the United States of America

24 23 22 • 5 6 7

CONTENTS

CHAPTER ONE

STAYING THE COURSE

> When the horn honked outside my house, out the door I ran. It was the church bus to pick me up and take me to church. I didn't realize I was a bus kid. I was just a kid who needed a ride to church. I didn't realize those bus workers and the awaiting teachers were investing their lives into mine and were endeavoring to disciple me in a way that would keep me on course for the rest of my life. I didn't realize that step by step they were laying a deep spiritual foundation in my life.

Josiah's father, Amon, was Israel's King. Unfortunately, Amon was not a godly man (2 Kings 21–23). As often happens with positions of power, the ability to participate in every type of impropriety money can buy lead to corruption and sinfulness. Perhaps Amon was not entirely to blame for his ungodly lifestyle, for his father, King Manasseh, was also an incredibly sinful man. Manasseh, Josiah's grandfather, was king of Israel for fifty-five years. Fifty-five years spent in disobedience to God. King Manasseh led in ungodly ways, and the people of Israel followed his sinful path. It was no wonder his son Amon, Josiah's father, lead in the same path. But King Josiah would be different.

Despite the wickedness of all of those around him, Josiah lived a godly life. Somehow, through the faithfulness of unknown leaders around him, he became a god-fearing young man who lived above reproach. Scripture doesn't tell us who impacted his life in a godly way. Perhaps it was his mother. More likely, the godly individual who influenced Josiah's life was one of his teachers or as we call them today, a kids ministry leader. Scripture doesn't tell us who helped to build the

> **STATISTICS SHOW THAT LARGE PERCENTAGES OF TEENAGERS ARE TURNING AWAY FROM THEIR FAITH IN CHRIST.**

deep spiritual foundation of Josiah's life, only that it was built. Somehow, by age eight when he became king, he already had a firmly established spiritual foundation. Someone had poured time and effort into the life of this young boy, introduced him to God, and built a lasting spiritual foundation that prepared him to be a godly king.

Are you laying spiritual foundations in the lives of your kids that are strong enough to last for a lifetime? Is your church taking kids through a systematic learning process designed to pass on a deep and lasting faith? Do the kids in your city have the opportunity to have spiritual foundations built into their lives?

A great percentage of church leaders say yes. They say they feature excellent ministries to kids. As well, most parents seem satisfied that they are passing on their biblical faith adequately. Unfortunately, statistics show otherwise. Statistics show that large percentages of teenagers are turning away from their faith in Christ. Researcher George Barna states, "Amazingly, less than half of the born-again teenagers (44 percent) said that they are absolutely committed to the Christian faith."[1] He goes on to say, "When asked to estimate the likelihood that they [Christian teens] will continue to participate in church life once they are living on their own, levels dip precipitously, to only about one out of every three teens [33 percent]."[2] These youth, growing up in Christian homes, have had the opportunity as kids to internalize the Christian faith, but have obviously lacked sufficient discipleship to make a lasting, life-changing impact upon their lives.[3] Unfortunately, discipleship began in these lives but wasn't sufficient to make them disciples who are willing and able to live for God their whole lives.

Christian youth who turn away from the faith has been a problem for the church as recorded throughout biblical history. Hezekiah was one of the godliest kings in the history of Judah. Second Kings chapter 19 records God's great deliverance through the faith and prayers of Hezekiah. Yet when his twelve-year-old son Manasseh took over as king, the Bible says the boy was wicked and did not serve God. Hezekiah, with all his importance and all his influence, somehow was not able to build a strong spiritual foundation in the life of his son. When it came time for his son to stand upon godly principles, he fell into sin instead.

> **LACK OF SPIRITUAL TRAINING AS KIDS PRODUCES TEENS WHO ARE SPIRITUALLY WEAK.**

If your heart, like mine, aches for the youth who are turning away from their faith, I think you'll agree with me that many churches and parents are not providing adequate spiritual training for their children. Lack of spiritual training as kids produces teens who are spiritually weak. Thus the statistics show generations of Christian teenagers relinquishing their faith when confronted with the challenges of life. We must not calculate successful kids ministries according to bodies present at church but by the number of kids who remain devoted to God throughout their lives.

Amon couldn't pass on a godly heritage to his son Josiah because Amon was not a godly man. Hezekiah failed to pass on a godly heritage to his son Manasseh. Non-Christian parents cannot pass on a Christian heritage to their children since they have none themselves. As well, many Christian parents seem to struggle building the spiritual foundation of their kids. That's why it is imperative for the church and Christian parents to partner together with a systematic, intentional plan for building spiritual foundations for their kids that are strong enough to last. The church must plan how to develop and disciple kids into mature believers who will choose to follow Jesus Christ for life.

FOUR INFLUENCES FOR A GODLY FAITH

In a study titled, "Factors in Youth and Young Adult Faith Experience and Development,"[4] the authors cite research on the small minority of youth who "stayed the course" throughout their Christian life. There were six common influences in the lives of these teens—*four occurred while they were kids.* These four were: (1) Christian faith deeply imbedded in their family; (2) at least three adult Christian mentors; (3) involved in ministry by age ten; and (4) going to a church defined as "cool" (i.e. relationships, worship service, engaging, etc.).[5] The teens who stayed the course had a strong spiritual foundation to sustain them—a foundation that was laid while they were kids.

The first of these four factors was the presence of a deep Christian faith in the family. They experienced faith demonstrated daily as part of the normal life of the family. Teenagers who lived their lives for God saw Christian faith acted out and displayed at home while they were kids. Family members had vital relationships with the Spirit of God. Trust in Jesus as Savior was evident. Obedience to the Word of God was the norm. These benefits and tremendous blessings are our goal for every child. That's why every KidMin leader must endeavor to positively influence the parents of their kids in order to strengthen the emphasis of biblical faith in the home.

The second factor was three adult mentors. For all of us who are KidMin leaders, what a responsibility this is—that the spiritual life of a child can be secured irrevocably by three mentoring leaders who take the time to indelibly impact the child. In a day when many emphasize the large group-ministry service to kids, the statistics tell us that a one-on-one relationship between a mentor and a child is one of the keys to lasting faith. Every KidMin leader has the potential to be one of these key mentors in the lives of kids.

Probably the most unique and surprising of the four factors mentioned in the study is involvement in ministry by age ten. Kids who actively serve God often find their life purpose and value while ministering in their church. Their self-esteem becomes tied to their service to God.

I was called at age twelve to be a pastor. Part of living for God was tied to serving in my church. There was never a consideration to do otherwise. Kids who use their talents to minister in the church begin to envision their future in service to God. This ministry becomes a spiritual cornerstone—an anchor to the faith. We will discuss ministry opportunities for kids in more detail in the chapter titled "Actively Serving." There we will present ministry opportunities as one of the eight goals that develops godly faith in kids.

Lastly, the fourth principle is the "cool" environment. This "cool" factor is one of the good trends of today. Churches are discovering the need to be cool, trendy, and inviting in order to attract kids and their families. An engaging place that attracts kids helps to hold them in place, as long as it is complemented with powerful services that provide the opportunity for kids to be impacted by God, His presence, and His anointed Word.

In today's society, the most difficult of these factors to implement isn't the family life, the cool setting, or even involvement in ministry. In most churches it's the willingness for volunteer leaders to give of themselves sufficiently to become mentors to the next generation.

You can find a plethora of books and articles on the subject of kids and spirituality. Many of these resources provide in-depth studies of age-level learning, intelligences, or learning styles—describing the different ways kids learn most effectively. Our goal here is to help parents and KidMin leaders understand how to build and measure the spiritual foundations of their kids.

In my extensive travels, I have come to recognize certain obvious signs of spiritual development in children. These signs indicate to me that certain steps of biblical training have occurred in the child's life and these form a solid spiritual foundation. This foundation doesn't just happen; it is built on purpose. It is built through the opportunities that loving parents and teachers and church leaders provide for the child. It is built through time spent discovering God. It is built through the power and presence of the Holy Spirit.

Parents and churches must take action to ensure their kids don't simply receive facts about faith in God, but develop a true and living relationship with God. Kids must discover God for themselves and learn to experience His presence throughout their lives. He is their hero.

They need to build their faith on Him. The goal of this book is to help kids ministry leaders, volunteers, and parents reach out to children and build a faith for the young that is strong enough to last their entire lives. A faith that is strong enough to take them through the most difficult challenges of life. A faith that is strong enough to keep them anchored in Christ.

Josiah had no godly parents, but godly leaders built into his young life a deep and abiding spiritual foundation. Let's consider a blueprint to help us develop a lasting spiritual faith in our kids.

CHAPTER TWO

A BLUEPRINT

Sitting in the branches of a tree, a twelve-year old boy found a private place to pray. He was totally unaware how unusual it was for a twelve-year-old boy to pass his time praying in a tree. While most boys were playing ball or catching frogs down at the river, he preferred to spend time in the presence of God—a gift he later realized came from spending time with his godly mother and godly teachers. Somehow, by the age of twelve, his young life was already built on a foundation of lasting faith.

God has always intended that parents and the church pass their spiritual heritage on to the next generation. In Joshua chapter four, twelve men hauled stones out from the middle of the Jordan River where the priests stood when the river stopped flowing. The Lord instructed these men to gather the stones and set them up as a memorial—a sign for the generations to follow. The stones signified the greatness and faithfulness of God.

God's plan was to build a memorial for the kids of the future, so they would not forget what He had done for their parents and their grandparents. God's blueprint guided the men as they stacked stones on a river bank for future generations of kids. Scripture states, "In the future, when your children ask you, 'What do these stones mean?' tell them that the flow of the Jordan was cut off before the ark of the covenant of the LORD. . . . These stones are to be a memorial to the people of Israel forever" (Josh. 4:6–7). God wanted future generations of kids to know of His power (stopping the Jordan River at flood stage), and His faithfulness (taking care of the needs of His people). He wanted the kids of the future to have the opportunity to know the God of the past as their God in the present. He wanted them to have a lasting faith that would allow them to live as spiritual champions. He wanted the kids to know Him.

It must be the plan and purpose of every church and every Christian parent to give kids the opportunity to discover the greatness of God, to introduce them to God at a young age and help them develop a relationship with Him. There must be a purposed plan—a blueprint.

The gathered stones served as a sign to spark questions from kids that would cause the adults to retell the story of God's greatness. These stories, which invoked an appreciation for God, provided a powerful opportunity to impact kid's lives by making them aware of His greatness and helping them discover His faithfulness. God planned for kids in future generations to experience divine moments with Him. These divine moments bring strength to kids' spiritual foundations and help them connect with their Lord and Savior, Jesus Christ. As the Israelites built an altar of stones, so we must build a spiritual foundation in the lives of our kids.

God has provided a blueprint to give kids every possible opportunity to discover and experience Him. This occurs through regular time spent with Him guided by godly parents and leaders.

Scripture clearly stresses the importance of passing one's spiritual heritage on to the next generation. Not only did God establish memorials to perpetuate spiritual faith, such as the stones previously mentioned, but He gave His people specific instructions about how to pass on their faith. Here is one passage that clearly exemplifies God's mandate for intentional, systematic exposure of kids to the Word of God and spiritual values:

> These commandments that I give you today are to be on your hearts. Impress them on your children. Talk about them when you sit at home and when you walk along the road, when you lie down and when you get up. Tie them as symbols on your hands and bind them on your foreheads. Write them on the doorframes of your houses and on your gates (Deut. 6:6–9).

The word *impress* is an emphatic word that means much more than just "to tell." A more accurate interpretation could read, "Share with them over and over the greatness of God and what He has done." Clearly, God was concerned that His people might neglect the responsibility of passing on spiritual faith to the next generation. In a day when parents and church leaders often decrease their discipleship efforts with kids, the Bible instructs us to do the opposite. Like a knife being sharpened by honing, God asks parents and leaders to sharpen their kids' biblical faith.

Research writer George Barna admits that he underestimated the importance of discipling kids. In his research, he was shocked to find the absolute necessity of adequately discipling individuals during childhood. He states,

> A person's moral foundations are generally in place by the time they reach age nine. Anyone who wishes to have a significant influence on the development of a person's moral and spiritual foundations had better exert that influence while the person is still open-minded and impressionable—in other words, while the person is still young.[6]

These key words, "open and impressionable," remind one that kids are "soft clay"—impressionable, pliable, and teachable. Proverbs 22:6 NKJV agrees, "Train up a child in the way he should go, and when he is old he will not depart from it." Barna's statistics bear this out when he states, "By age thirteen, your spiritual identity is largely set in place,"[7] and, "In essence, what you believe by the time you are thirteen is what you will die believing."[8] Unless God miraculously intervenes later in their life, childhood is where kid's spiritual foundations are built.

The failure of teenagers to live the faith they seemed to possess as children points back to inadequate step-by-step discipleship while they were young. It must be the goal of Christian parents and KidMin leaders to share their faith with their kids day after day. May our love

> **UNLESS GOD MIRACULOUSLY INTERVENES LATER IN THEIR LIFE, CHILDHOOD IS WHERE KID'S SPIRITUAL FOUNDATIONS ARE BUILT.**

for God become the love of our children for God. As a church we must endeavor to build a deep spiritual foundation for our kids by helping them know God in a deep and personal way.

What is the blueprint for a healthy physical body? We can easily identify certain factors that will produce health for the body: nutrients, vitamins, proteins, and calcium are building blocks of proper diet. A balance of these and other nutrients combined with regular exercise and adequate sleep produces healthy minds and bodies. Obviously there are exceptions to these rules, but in general kids who eat only junk food are apt to become fat, lethargic, or weak. Kids who lack vitamins or rest will lack energy to function properly. Clearly we have a blueprint for a healthy body; skip proper rest, exercise, and nutrition and there will be a negative result.

The spiritual growth of a child depends upon a blueprint as well. The child needs a regular diet of spiritual nutrients every day. The parents and the church must be committed to the spiritual growth of the child. The church can't have a fast-food mentality of giving every child a spiritual snack. The church must have a philosophy—a blueprint—that each and every time a child attends a classroom, a small group, or a large group, that child will receive a balanced diet of spiritual nutrition. The family must faithfully attend church to provide children with as many opportunities as possible to learn about God. The church must provide well-trained teachers who are determined to build a strong spiritual foundation in every kid.

Bible passages that instruct parents about a daily spiritual life for their child show intentionality: "When you sit at home and when you walk along the road, when you lie down and when you get up" (Deut. 6:7). These instructions focused on every hour of the day, whether sitting at home or getting ready for bed. However, these instructions were given to the entire body of God's people who moved together as a nomadic group. So when God instructed them to talk when they walked along the road, (v. 7), His instructions were for the whole believing community. Every man and woman was responsible to pass spiritual truths on to all the kids. By contrast, it's almost a foreign concept today to think that the entire church is responsible to pass on spiritual faith to the next generation. But this mandate isn't a calling of just a few—it is for the entire church, especially since many kids are without Christian parents. The church

> **IT'S ALMOST A FOREIGN CONCEPT TODAY TO THINK THAT THE ENTIRE CHURCH IS RESPONSIBLE TO PASS ON SPIRITUAL FAITH TO THE NEXT GENERATION.**

of today must choose its own blueprint on how the kids under its care receive a solid biblical foundation.

Clearly God intended that every new generation of kids learn to know Him and to follow His commandments. He assured the people of Israel that if the kids heard about God, they would learn to revere Him.

Please note one key difference in the passage below. God not only cares about the church passing on a spiritual heritage to the kids of believers; God insists that the church be equally concerned about developing a spiritual life in the hearts of unsaved kids.

> Assemble the people—men, women and children, and the *foreigners* residing in your towns—so they can listen and learn to fear the LORD your God and follow carefully all the words of this law. *Their children, who do not know this law, must hear it and learn to fear the LORD your God....*
> (Deut. 31:12–13, emphasis added)

What do these verses mean to us today? God instructs the church to reach the lost kids who don't know about Him. The mandate for the church is that we must take every opportunity possible to reach the lost kids living nearby. Sadly, these kids are often neglected. Churches are so busy with activities designed for the church-going family that they fail to go out and reach the kids whose families do not attend church. There seems to be a mentality that the lost must come to the church. But God wants kids who don't know Him or the stories of His miraculous deeds to receive spiritual training through the church as a surrogate spiritual parent.

BLUEPRINTS FOR THE CHURCH AND FOR PARENTS

The first step for building the spiritual foundations of kids is to decide on a blueprint. This book will give you the basis of that blueprint. Your blueprint should be something like the following:

THE CHURCH

1. *We desire that in our church every child would have the opportunity to discover God and His Word through the guidance of trained and qualified KidMin leaders through avenues of both large and small groups.*

2. *It is our goal that every child impacted by our discipleship efforts will choose to live for God the rest of his/her life. These children will be spiritually sound enough through knowing God, His Word, and through genuine relationships with KidMin leaders and Christian friends to resist the attacks of the Enemy that will come against them.*

3. *It is our plan to invest our best efforts in discipling kids within our church family and evangelizing the lost kids of our community.*

4. *As a church we pledge to support and encourage the discipleship of kids through adequate facilities, financing, quality trained leaders, and pastoral support.*

5. *It is our goal to disciple kids through the eight goals of discipleship. These goals include raising up kids who are: powerful in prayer, responsive in worship, Spirit empowered, biblically fluent, actively serving, bold in faith, giving selflessly, and living like Christ.*

THE PARENT

1. *I determine that my kids will discover God, personally know God, and grow their spiritual foundation through time spent with me at home showing them my relationship with God in my everyday life.*
2. *I determine that my life will serve as a godly example of a Christian's dependence upon God and obedience to His Word.*
3. *I will give my kids every opportunity to be impacted in godly ways through regular attendance at a church that is determined to invest in the spiritual growth of my kids.*
4. *It is my goal that my kids will be so adequately disciplined in their Christian walk that they will choose to live for God the rest of lives. They will be spiritually sound enough through their relationship with God, their belief in His Word, and through the genuine relationships of KidMin leaders and friends to resist the many attacks of the Enemy that will come against them in the years to come.*
5. *It is my desire that my life will positively impact both my kids, as well as other kids not fortunate enough to have a Christian parent so they will have the opportunity to know Jesus as their personal Savior.*
6. *It is my goal that my kids and other kids I impact will grow through the eight goals of discipleship. These goals include raising up kids who are: powerful in prayer, responsive in worship, Spirit empowered, biblically fluent, actively serving, bold in faith, giving selflessly, and living like Christ.*

BOTH PARENTS AND THE CHURCH MUST TAKE SPIRITUAL RESPONSIBILITY FOR CHILDREN.

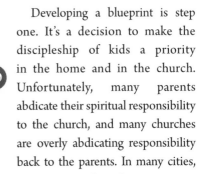

Developing a blueprint is step one. It's a decision to make the discipleship of kids a priority in the home and in the church. Unfortunately, many parents abdicate their spiritual responsibility to the church, and many churches are overly abdicating responsibility back to the parents. In many cities, kids without Christian parents have no one to give them the opportunity to know Christ. A friend of mine told how some people in his town picked him up and brought him to church when he was seven. He accepted Christ, loved the church, and grew spiritually. But then the people suddenly stopped picking him up and bringing him to church. From that point on, he grew up without Christ, without any influence from the church. He went through many tough seasons of life. Later he found Christ again in his college years, but he told me he often wonders why those people stopped taking him to church.

Church leaders and parents may also assume too much. They assume a child who attends church once a week will automatically develop a lasting faith. Often children's services are overly designed to attract and entertain rather than introduce a deep and lasting faith. Parents assume the church is adequately discipling their kids; and the church assumes the parents are doing this. Both parents and the church must take spiritual responsibility for children. Each must determine that their goal and purpose is to insure that every child under their care will grow a lasting and sincere faith that will carry them through the rest of their lives. We must also realize that for many kids, the church is the only source of discipling in the child's life. May this passage be the spiritual anchor to your blueprint.

> We will tell the next generation the praiseworthy deeds of
> the LORD, his power, and the wonders he has done . . . so
> the next generation would know them, even the children

yet to be born, and they in turn would tell their children. Then they would put their trust in God and would not forget his deeds but would keep his commands. (Ps. 78:4, 6–7)

Tips for Parents

Passing on your faith can seem like a daunting task. You may ask, "How is this done?" The first step is to determine that you will make it a priority. You wouldn't be reading this book if that wasn't important to you.

Make it your goal to tell your kids about God. Tell them how you came to know Christ. Share with them how God has answered your prayers. Play verbal games with your kids: "Let's all think of reasons God is good." "He is good because He watches over us." "He is good because He loves us." Your kids will first *serve* the God you love. Later they will learn to *love* the God you love.

Tips for Kids Ministry Leaders

Determine that each kid is worthy of your investment. Learn the background of each kid. Know which ones do and don't have both parents. Know which ones have Christian parents. Spiritually adopt each child; determine that they are your spiritual kids and treat them as such. Don't forget to do the things parents should do: talk about your faith, your God, how you were saved, and what God has done for you. Kids will first *serve* the God you serve and then will *love* the God you love.

Create your own blueprint—a pact in writing that states your purpose to impact the next generation.

BRING THE CHILDREN TO JESUS

As the young boy prayed in the fork of the tree, God spoke to his heart, guiding the boy on the path his life would take. I was that boy. As I prayed in the fork of that tree God asked if I would be willing to be a pastor someday. I told Him yes. That was many years ago. I have served God in fulltime ministry for many years. I have found that the majority of

Christian leaders can place their initial walk with God from childhood.

That's where my calling to ministry began. My father wasn't particularly pleased with my choice, but he saw God working in my life. Our family lived through many difficult times, but God used all these experiences to build a lasting faith in my life.

Jesus told His disciples to let the children come to Him. "Let the little children come to me, and do not hinder them, for the kingdom of God belongs to such as these" (Mark 10:14). The scene that day often evokes an image of Jesus comfortably teaching the people on a hillside and women standing in line with their children to ask for an audience with Him. Having worked in children's ministries for over thirty years, I can guarantee the scene wasn't nearly that calm and sedated. Imagine the disciples holding back a thronging crowd of people who wanted to get close to Jesus. The crowd includes mothers with kids of all ages. Picture young kids squeezing through the disciples' legs, shouting, "Come, Mama, I see Him! I see Him!" Despite the disciples' best efforts, kids broke through the line to be close to Jesus. When Jesus said, "Let the children come," the floodgates opened as dozens of kids rushed forward, pushing to get close to Him. Hours may have passed as mother after mother brought her kids to Jesus. The mothers wanted Jesus to touch their kids, but Jesus did far more—He welcomed them. To the disciples, kids were an interruption, but to Jesus, kids were of prime importance.

The words of Jesus in Matthew make His thoughts even more clear. "If anyone gives even a cup of cold water to one of these little ones who is my disciple, truly I tell you, that person will certainly not lose their reward" (Matt. 10:42).

Tips for Parents
Jesus wanted kids to be close so they could know Him and He could know them. The disciples didn't take this seriously, and Jesus was indignant with them. He said, "Bring the children to me." We must provide opportunities for kids to be with Jesus at home and at church. Children develop a sincere godly faith as they discover God and His Spirit by spending time with Him. Tell your kids of your early

spiritual foundation. How did you discover God? How did you come to know more about Him? Tell them of your struggles, mistakes, and learning processes. These interactions don't have to happen in a rigid environment or at a scheduled time. Simply share with your kids whenever you're with them and feel it's appropriate. When you're traveling in the car, you might share "talk time" instead of video time, music time, game time, etc.

I also encourage you to attend church faithfully and give your kids this prime opportunity to discover more about the gospel message while interacting with other kids and with spiritual mentors.

Tips for Kids Ministry Leaders

Billy's parents were getting a divorce. Like most divorces, it was difficult on the family. Billy was there in court. As an eleven-year-old boy, he didn't have the right to make the decision whether he would live with his mother or his father. The judge, however, was interested in his opinion. If Billy wanted to stay with his father as opposed to his mother that might swing the judge's decision. The judge asked Billy. "Billy, where would you like to live?" Billy responded in words that surprised everyone: "With Mr. Charlie! He's my teacher at church."

As KidMin leaders, we often underestimate the importance of our influence on the lives of kids. Often, the most important reason a child comes to church is to see their KidMin leader; this is more important than the activities, the games, the snacks, or anything else. Kids are looking for that individual who knows their name, who notices them, smiles at them, and speaks affirmation into their lives. It can be as simple as saying, "There's Samantha, the girl with all of those cute freckles." Or, "Raphael, let me see those muscles of yours. They seem to get bigger every week." Kids love to be noticed. When you notice them, they love you. After they love you, they will learn to love your God.

CHAPTER THREE

BUILDING DEEP FAITH

Troy and Tonya came to our church because of a kids crusade. A hundred new kids came as visitors that year, and Troy and Tonya's family were some of many who continued to attend our church as we followed up on them. Both kids were quiet but talented. Both continued to grow in their walk with God.

Shane also came to our church through outreach. Soon he and his family found the Lord. Shane, an energetic, fun-loving young man, loved to be the life of the party.

Trent and his parents attended our church. He loved the sound system, computer system, any system you could name, he wanted to run it.

These four kids eventually formed a part of our ministry team. They were involved in our summer outreaches and our ministry to other kids. Together they grew into a tightly knit ministry team. Together they found mentors willing to invest in their lives, and their faith grew by leaps and bounds.

Kids have a spiritual capacity far beyond what many people think possible. In Samuel chapter 3, the young boy Samuel received a prophetic word from God. Many would speculate that to hear God's voice at such a young age, he must have been a "one-in-a-million" super-spiritual kid. Yet, it isn't uncommon for kids to hear God's voice and to called by Him at a young age. I shared earlier how God called me into ministry when I was twelve. One study in our denomination shows a large number of missionaries being called to ministry while they were kids. A great many pastors also report having heard God's voice as kids, calling them to full-time ministry. When given the opportunity, kids discover God and learn to hear, recognize, and respond to His voice. They have the potential for deep faith.

History records that at the turn of the twentieth century, numerous kids were mightily used by God through healings, infillings of the Spirit, visions, prophetic words, miracles, and great abilities to share the gospel. We have seen God move on thousands of kids to baptize them in the Holy Spirit and call them to ministry. Kids regularly experience miraculously answers to their prayers. Spiritual fervor isn't limited to kids in the Bible; it happens to kids today as they experience powerful "divine moments" that change their lives forever.

My wife, Mary, and I have had the opportunity to speak at kid's camps and conventions across the United States. We have witnessed God move powerfully upon kids as they worship, pray, and receive Bible teaching. Camps serve as a vital experience for kids in spiritual formation. KidMin leaders prepare for camp expecting the kids to receive great things from God. These expectations, coupled with biblical preaching, ample time to worship, prayer, and lingering at the altar, create an environment where kids respond to the presence of God. They respond with recommitment, worship, hearing God's voice, and answering calls to full-time service.

Unfortunately, churches often have lower expectations for kids during weekly services or classes. Low expectations are reflected by the lack of time set aside for prayer, worship, preaching, and altar response. Instead, one often finds an entertainment mindset in many churches that diminishes the opportunity for the supernatural.

Judy, a fifth grade boys Sunday school teacher, felt strongly that God had instructed her to introduce each boy to the infilling of the Holy Spirit during their fifth grade year. For twenty years, nearly every boy in her classroom was filled with the Spirit—some at home and some at church, but each in their own place and time. Her expectations helped to bring about great spiritual results in the lives of these boys.

God's Spirit will move among kids in churches that provide opportunities for this to happen. KidMin leaders must expect that kids will receive more than a "spiritual nugget" or a "thought for the day"

> **GOD'S SPIRIT WILL MOVE AMONG KIDS IN CHURCHES THAT PROVIDE OPPORTUNITIES FOR THIS TO HAPPEN.**

when they come to church. Kids are impacted spiritually when KidMin leaders set aside time for them to experience God, touch God, and evaluate His Word in their lives. If leaders set aside time in services and classrooms and teach kids to seek God, He will respond. Each encounter with kids should prompt leaders to ask, "Did the kids have an opportunity today to discover God? Did they get a chance to know Him more? Did they experience the Spirit of God in their lives?"

Parents enhance the learning experience of their kids by talking with them about their own relationship with God: when the parent hears His voice, what He says, what they sense His Word is saying. If parents are willing to allow times to share spiritual experiences with their kids, the kids will ask questions and their faith will grow.

Often leaders mistakenly endeavor to overly entertain kids. This is unnecessary. Kids in the presence of God respond to Him. In this regard, kids pastor Randy Christensen states,

> If we operate with the supernatural empowering and guidance of the Holy Spirit, children will be captivated! No one can ignore a true move of God! When children sense the presence of God during worship, when they lay hands on a friend and see a healing occur, when the unsaved walk the aisle in response to the gospel, one will not have a problem maintaining children's attention![9]

Kids lives are changed when they have time to discover God and learn to hear His voice. Entertainment is a tool to attract kids to come to church and to entice them to come back. It's the vehicle for providing kids with opportunities to experience God. A kids' service isn't a circus or a show; it's an opportunity for kids to meet with God. A great author, Scotty May, states: "We have the privilege of providing opportunities for children to come face to face with the living God—in other words, to experience God, not simply learn about God."[10]

During the last thirty years, Mary and I have used a wide variety of media and tools to minister to kids, but we have always felt that the methods were secondary to the message. Yes, creativity invites kids to learn, but only the presence of God can change lives. Kids are attracted to church when they know it's going to be fun, and they return to church because of the fun and great relationships with other kids and KidMin leaders. But kids' lives *change* because of the power of God. Anything less than the power of God in kids' classrooms and services will be for naught.

Historically, kids have received a mighty infilling of the power of God. This infilling continues today in churches that make provisions for it to happen. Kids can't wait to grow up—both physically and spiritually. If leaders or parents expect to build a deep and solid spiritual foundation in kid's lives, they must be intentional about it. God has created kids with a sincere hunger to know Him, and they will respond to opportunities to be in His presence.

As I mentioned in the introduction of this chapter, Troy, Trent, Tonya, and Shane ministered together on the same ministry team. Although they came from different backgrounds—some from Christian homes and some from non-Christian homes—soon their parents all attended church. The faith of these four kids flourished. They were all involved in ministry. They were all excited about their "cool" church. And they had all found godly mentors who invested in their lives. Today Troy is an Army chaplain, Trent is a pastor, Shane is a youth pastor, and Tonya is a pastor's wife. All four are living for God—statistically an impossibility when only one of the four should have maintained a strong faith. But with dedicated parents and Christian mentors, they built a strong faith that has lasted the tests of time.

God is still calling kids, empowering kids, and raising up kids. As KidMin leaders and parents we need to make it our purpose to build a lasting faith in the next generation.

Tips for Parents

Kids are far more capable than we think. Don't be afraid to be honest with them. In future chapters, as we examine prayer, you'll realize the importance of prayer in building a child's faith. Encourage your kids to pray for their own needs and for the needs of others. Then watch them get excited when they see answers to those prayers. As kids practice intercessory prayer they will build sturdy faith in God.

When a child says that God spoke to them, don't take it lightly. Treat it as a genuine experience and examine it in light of Scripture. Use the Bible to teach your children how to guard their hearts and resist temptation. Let them see how you use God's Word as a guideline for your life, and they will learn to do the same.

Tips for Kids Ministry Leaders

You are mentors who are developing relationships with kids. Aim to build a relationship that will last a lifetime. Some day you will think back to the childhood of kids who are serving God as adults. You will have the opportunity to say, "I was a part of their success!" You have the opportunity to influence these adults as kids when they are soft clay. You can minister to them when their spirits are most open to the things of God. If you fail to take advantage of the opportunities God has given you to impress their spirits with the presence of God, there may come a day when they will become hardened to the things of God.

At times I've noticed one of the KidMin leaders at our church talking excitedly with a teenager who has just won an award. The young person shares the accomplishment with great pride. Several times when I assumed the teenager was a relative, I have been pleasantly surprised to learn that the adult was actually a KidMin leader when the teenager was in third grade. What makes a teenager want to share a special event with a KidMin leader from childhood? It's called relationship. The relationships leaders develop with kids at age nine can last a lifetime! Remember, you can earn a lifetime of mentorship through a year's worth of relationship building.

Make sure your ministry is a balance of fun and discipleship. If kids say they had fun, that's a win because they will likely be back. If kids say they were touched by God—that's a huge win! They are on a journey toward lifelong and sincere faith.

CHAPTER FOUR

THE CHILDREN'S MENTOR

Howard honked the horn of the bus. It was the sound we had been waiting for. A lot had happened since I sat in the fork of the tree and talked to God. My mom had gotten sick and gone away. Dad had divorced her and married another woman, which meant I picked up another brother and sister in the deal. Now six of us piled onto the bus each Sunday and Wednesday, scurrying to get the best seat.

I was excited to get on that bus because it meant I would get to see my Sunday school teacher, Pearl Gange. What can I tell you about her? Through my young eyes she was just about the smartest person I knew. She let me ask all kinds of questions and did her best to answer them.

Both she and Howard Cummings, the bus driver who was also the pastor, loved God and loved me. Through the years, my five brothers and sisters and I had several bus workers and teachers. Each one had a part in guiding us on our spiritual journeys.

Scripture teaches that God commands us to intentionally pass our spiritual faith to the next generation. Kids receive insight, direction, and power from God when they receive proper instruction and are given opportunities to pray and worship and grow in faith. The mandate of every KidMin leader compels them to offer kids the best things from God—to build their spiritual foundations strong and deep by introducing them to an intimate relationship with the Lord.

The spiritual expectations of KidMin leaders directly correlate to the spiritual outcomes that kids receive. The authors of *Children Matter* explain that teachers "have the privilege of providing opportunities for children to come face to face with the living God."[11] In other words, kids see many more answers to prayer when they have ample opportunities to pray. Kids sense the presence of God in worship when given regular opportunities to worship. Teachers must ensure that kids have opportunities with God every time they gather; anything less becomes a mere exercise in "church."

Take a moment and think of one person who had a significant impact on your life. Recall what it was like to be in their presence. If you were in a classroom, put yourself back in that classroom again for a moment. If it was at an event, imagine being there again. Now choose one word that you would use to describe that person. Write it down. _____

Often Christians who have grown up in one church can point to a particular individual who had the greatest influence in their lives while they were young. When asked to choose one word to describe these mentors, these influential individuals are often described with these terms: listener, love, available, reliable, guide, coach, mentor, caring, faithful, etc. What word did you choose? Rarely do individuals choose the word handsome, pretty, talented, or even smart. They choose relational terms like friend, faithful, affirming, gracious, or kind. Leaders become mentors with lasting impact as they lovingly care for those they teach. Mentors lead by example and in relationship. As KidMin leaders, they faithfully guide their students. As parents or grandparents, they set a daily example of Christian life.

Recently I attended the funeral of a friend I can only describe as a giant of a man. He had a giant love for people. He invested in them, spoke to them, affirmed them, and cared for them. Person after person stood at the funeral and shared how this man made their lives better. They didn't talk about his wisdom or his preaching or teaching, although he was gifted in all those things. What they did mention was his kind heart. He shared his heart with me and made my life better. He lived his life like Jesus did, and we all saw that, felt it, and became better because of it. Literally thousands of young people, leaders, pastors, and guys like me include him on their list of mentors. Keith Elder was a spiritual giant of a man.

Spurgeon writes, "Before you can teach children, you must get the silver key of kindness to unlock their hearts, and so secure their

> **A GOOD TEACHER DEVELOPS A LOVING, CARING RELATIONSHIP WITH HIS OR HER STUDENTS AND EARNS THE RIGHT TO ESCORT THEM INTO THE PRESENCE OF GOD.**

attention."[12] A good teacher develops a loving, caring relationship with his or her students and earns the right to escort them into the presence of God. That's what Keith did. Whether a teacher, leader, or parent, each person is responsible to help kids experience face-to-face encounters with God and the Holy Spirit.

Influential teachers lead by example, changing kids forever by providing opportunities for their spiritual foundations to grow deep. It can be difficult to have this type of influence in a large group setting. It's difficult to earn the title "friend" if a child is merely one in many. It's also difficult to show love and kindness if you only give kids a quick handshake on the way in or out. That's the value of a small group. Churches must provide kids with both large and small group services. Kids need time with adults for relationships and mentorships to grow. In a small group adults model "Jesus with skin on." KidMin leaders who are willing to exemplify Christ with their own lives will help to grow a sincere godly faith in the lives of kids.

Year after year, we six kids ran out of the house and onto the church bus. Today all six of us continue our relationship with Christ. Raising godly families, we all are passing on the godly faith that was freely given to us. Each of us can point to leaders in that church who became our personal mentors to show us the way.

Tips for Parents

Kids need to attend a church that intentionally offers experiences to build biblical faith through quality relationships with adults. Quiz your kids on the way home. Find out what they are learning. Visit the classrooms and kids' church services regularly. Make sure your kids are receiving a nourishing spiritual diet.

At home, check your "spiritual" diet. What are you investing in your child's spiritual development? Are you providing your child with the valuable experience of Christian camp? Many parents send their kids to soccer camp, basketball camp, cheerleading camp, music camp, etc., and claim that time and money have run out when it's time to send them to church camp. Invest wisely and generously in your child's spiritual development. Put church camp at the top of your camp list. It will make an enormous difference in the spiritual faith of your child.

Make it a priority in your home to spend time with God. This can be a challenge for busy parents, but parents who want to develop spiritually healthy kids will find the time. Perhaps the best time is just before bed. The kids don't want to go to sleep anyway, so make it a time to read a Bible story and ask a few leading questions such as: "Was the person in the story scared? Did he trust God? What would you have done?"

You are the gauge by which your kids will grow in Christ. Your faith, your faithfulness to the house of God, and your willingness to talk with your kids about the things of God will establish their spiritual foundations for life. Yes, kids can stray, but you are the gauge that determines how much spiritual DNA is woven into the fabric of their being.

Tips for Kids Ministry Leaders

Now more than ever the church needs kids ministry leaders who choose to remain faithful to the task God has given them. Often experienced volunteers decide it is time for someone else to step into their position just when God has given them the experience and the knowledge to change kid's lives as never before. Leaders go through seasons of life when their ministry may turn from toddlers, to elementary, to middle school, but God has instructed leaders to be faithful and multiply the kingdom until He comes. He is coming quickly. Strive to make a difference in the lives of kids. You will have no regrets when you see kids who have grown to serve God.

CHAPTER FIVE

EIGHT GOALS TO BUILD STRONG FAITH

A farmer hired a farmhand to plant a field of corn. So the farmhand planted it, but not like he should have. Sure, the corn sprouted and began to grow, but as it got nearly waist high, it began to turn yellow and died. The farmhand—planting the corn as quickly and easily as he could—had failed to fertilize the ground. The soil lacked nutrients, and the plants lacked inner strength. Many of the corn stalks withered and died. As weeks passed, weeds grew up and choked much of the corn, causing more of it to wither and die. The farmhand had failed to protect the soil with weed preventer. Unhindered, the weeds multiplied, grew, and choked out the plants. Finally, a storm came and blew down most of the remaining corn. The farmhand had failed to till the soil before planting. Without soft earth, the roots couldn't tunnel deep and anchor the plants. The roots were shallow, and the wind overturned the stalks.

The farmer worked feverishly night and day pulling weeds, laying down fertilizer, and propping up cornstalks, in hopes that the crop would regain its health and grow. In the end, he could salvage only a small portion of his crop. The harvest would have been much richer if the farmhand had tilled the soil, fertilized it, and laid down weed-preventing barriers to protect the young crop. Unfortunately, his goal had been to simply plant corn—not to plant corn that would grow strong, bear fruit, and thrive.

Like farmers who must take care to ensure the health of their crops, parents and KidMin leaders must take steps early in the lives of kids to ensure quality long-term results. The farmhand in the story represents individuals who fail to build a solid spiritual foundation in the lives of kids. Rather than develop spiritual roots that grow deep into the soil, these kids are inadequately prepared for the challenges of life that lay ahead. The farmer represents the youth leader who, although working feverishly, would have had much greater fruit if he had taken steps to ensure a bountiful harvest.

This illustration reminds us of the story Jesus told about the lost sheep, referring to the "good shepherd" and the "hired hand" (see John 10:11–14). The good shepherd knows his sheep by name, and they know him. The good shepherd invests himself in the sheep and is even willing to die for the sheep. Not so for the hired hand. He puts forth the minimum effort and that is all. Jesus asks us to choose whether we will be a good shepherd or simply a hired hand.

Parents must endeavor to plant a godly foundation in their kids, and the church has a responsibility to develop quality individuals with a desire to reach and disciple young lives. The statistics stated earlier show that far too many kids in our churches lose out with God as teens due to weak spiritual roots that were not sufficiently developed when they were young. These teens received insufficient preparation to withstand the ungodly influences and winds of conformity. The key to reverse this downward trend is for the church to intentionally invest the most qualified individuals in ministry to kids. Tedd Tripp calls the process of investing in a child's spiritual life "shepherding the heart."[13] As good shepherds, KidMin leaders share the responsibility to ensure that each young lamb receives all the care necessary to follow the Master Shepherd forever.

Let's not forget that kids are far more spiritually capable than we often admit. Leaders tend to treat kids childishly, expecting too little of them—far less than God intended. Remember, Jesus spoke of a kid's faith when He said adults must "receive the kingdom of God like a little child" (Mark 10:15). Leaders must consider the age of the child, of course, but astute leaders constantly create a teaching environment that allows for spiritual insights to drill deep at any age.

Many helpful resources teach church leaders and parents about age-appropriate types of learning that kids can and should receive. These books address "scopes and sequences" and systematic plans for teaching Christian principles in a step-by-step approach. Although there are many spiritual steps in a child's spiritual development, this book concentrates on eight specific goals of spiritual development. Each of these goals serves as a building block for the spiritual foundation of kids.

Here are the eight goals:

1. Powerful in Prayer
2. Responsive in Worship
3. Biblically Fluent
4. Spirit Empowered
5. Actively Serving
6. Bold in Faith
7. Giving Selflessly
8. Living Like Christ

Each one entails a myriad of spiritual lessons that can build a core of inner strength, knowledge, and spiritual fortitude that will remain throughout their lives.

Another farmhand was given the same job—to plant a field of corn for the farmer. He did so carefully, knowing that although his primary job was to plant and nurture the young plants, he wouldn't fully accomplish his job unless the plants continued to grow and thrive all the way through harvest.

First, he tilled the soil so the young roots would grow deep and strong. He fertilized so the crops would have all the nutrients for healthy growth. Then he added weed killer to guard against the weeds that he knew would eventually strive to come and choke the young plants. The farmer was pleased to see that as weeks passed the corn continued to thrive. The farmhand continued to care for the young crop and it flourished.

One night, a storm came and blew down much of the crops in the fields nearby, but this field stood strong. The farmer found a few plants here and there damaged by the storm, but the majority of the crop stood the test of the storm. In time he harvested a bountiful crops.

Tips for Parents

Depth is the key. How do you develop depth in your child? First, start early. It's never too early to talk with your child about God. Preschoolers love to pray. One little child praying with a "stethoscope" placed it on her chest and declared, "I hear Jesus down there." Obviously, the child was learning the whole concept of having Jesus in her heart. She knew He was in her life somewhere.

Let your kids experience God. Make sure they are faithful in church and other church events. Talk about your faith. Pray with your kids. Talk with them about what the Holy Spirit is saying to them. Affirm their young spiritual thoughts.

Read, read, and read quality Christian books to your children. And read books that will help you as a godly parent. Bible bookstores provide plenty of helpful books on Christian parenting. Read those books. Read them on your break. Read them before bed. It's okay if it takes a while to read a book. You absorb it more that way. Books are full of great ideas for parents.

Shepherd the heart of your kids. I like that idea. God has given you, the parent, the job of shepherding your child's heart. One way to build spiritual resilience is to ask your kids questions, then talk about the answers. Here are some examples:

1. Have you met Jesus as your Savior? What is He like?
2. Would you like to know how I met Jesus?
3. How will you respond if someone makes fun of you for being a Christian?
4. Has God answered your prayers?
5. Has God ever spoken to you?
6. Has God ever done a miracle for someone you know?

7. How do you know the Bible is true?
8. What if a friend asks you to help them become a Christian?
9. What will you say if someone asks you to do something wrong?
10. Have you ever felt God? When?

Tips for Kids Ministry Leaders

Strive to be the type of leader who wants a "crop" that lasts. Do everything in your power to plant the Word of God deep in the hearts of your kids. Take the time to make sure their spiritual roots are growing deep. Choose a curriculum that has a strong scope and sequence. Choose a curriculum that is designed to teach kids lessons that will help them to stand for Christ. Decide to impact both kids in your church who have Christian parents and unsaved kids in your community.

Strive to use the eight goals we will share in the next few chapters to build spiritual faith in your kids. Each goal is an important step that will help your kids develop deep spiritual roots. They will help to insure that all the spiritual nutrients are growing healthy biblical faith that will enable kids to stand the test of time as difficulties of the future test their faith.

CHAPTER SIX

POWERFUL IN PRAYER

Hundreds of books have been written about prayer. Prayer is multifaceted and powerful. Kids need to learn the many avenues of prayer, including prayer for help, strength, courage, wisdom, healing, comfort, salvation, direction, etc. When children pray, their prayers provide a glimpse of their spiritual depth. Their prayers reveal their relationship with God, their faith, their values, and their expectations. Whether kids pray before bed, at the altar, in church, or at home, their prayers clarify their understanding of God. This is especially true when their prayers are answered. As is true of every believer, kids learn the power of prayer when their prayers are answered. Kids can intercede powerfully for others.

There are several lessons kids learn when they pray and God miraculously answers. First, they learn that God hears them when they pray because He answered their prayer. Second, since He answered, they realize God is alive. They now know that God is real. Third, they understand that God cares about them because He was willing to answer their prayer. Finally, they realize that God is powerful because He was mighty enough to answer their prayer in a supernatural way. Prayer is a mighty avenue for kids to discover God, His love for them, and His greatness.

Not only do kids discover God through His answers to their prayers, they also experience Him through His presence when they pray. Through prayer, kids quickly ascertain the actual presence of God. They sense His presence, His closeness, and His being. In the midst of His closeness, they discover His voice. They respond when He whispers quietly into their hearts. These discoveries of God through prayer become the foundation of a lifelong relationship with God.

Though it takes a lifetime to learn about prayer, it is simple to teach children to pray and they seem to excel at praying right from the start. Kids

LEADERS BEST MODEL PRAYER BY SHOWING A LOVE FOR PRAYER.

most effectively learn to pray by watching the leaders they love pray. Leaders best model prayer by showing a love for prayer. Adults who have built relationships with the kids have the greatest influence when modeling prayer. As kids hear adults, their parents, or leaders pray, they learn how and when to pray!

As the KidMin leader exemplifies a passion to pray, kids learn the joy of prayer. Prayer gives kids the opportunity to experience divine moments with God. When God answers their prayers—no matter how small or insignificant—they discover the "realness" of God. One young girl, when looking at a chart of all the prayer requests of the kids over the past few months and all the stars where God had answered, said: "Wow, God really does answer prayers, doesn't He?" This child rode to church on the church bus and didn't have the advantage of a Christian parent reinforcing her spiritual values. That chart in her Sunday school class was visual proof that God answers prayer, He cares, and He hears.

We teach prayer by example, as well as by experience. Most kids are naturally open to prayer, and given the opportunity to pray they learn to love it. Opportunities for prayer might include: opening the classroom in prayer, praying for the sick, praying for missionaries, praying for the lost, or praying at the altar. Author Dick Gruber emphasizes this when he says, "All of these experiences further the spiritual nurture of the children which is the purpose of the church."[14]

A wise KidMin leader gives kids opportunities to pray aloud in front of others. Boldness grows when kids pray aloud. You can help them overcome any hesitancy if you affirm them when they pray in front of others. This builds their confidence. Every prayer spoken from a righteous heart before God is a wonderful prayer. Let me add an important note here: Never force a child to pray out loud or embarrass them by asking them to pray. Always let kids volunteer to pray out loud. Praying in front of others can be a traumatic experience for a child, and this could prevent them from attending kids ministry for fear they will have to stand in front of others to pray.

You can include kids in various times of prayer such as prayer circles, prayer partners, prayer lines, silent prayers, or corporate prayers. These types of prayers give kids opportunities to learn to pray in different settings. It also allows them to hear the prayer needs of others so they can rejoice with answers to the prayers.

We teach prayer by example, by experience, and by testimony. When kids have received an answer to prayer, let them testify about it. This gives other kids a chance to hear when God answers their prayers for their friends. It ignites their desire to pray more. The more they talk to the Spirit of God and see His answers to their prayers, the more they understand the power of prayer and the deeper their faith grows.

It's also important to the spiritual foundation of kids for them to hear adults share testimonies of God's miracles and answers to prayer. Deuteronomy 11:2 says, "Your children were not the ones who saw." In other words, those kids were not alive to see the miracles of God when He delivered their parents; the kids could only learn about the miracles when adults shared testimonies of God's greatness. That's why God instructed His people to communicate His great deeds so that the faith of the kids might grow.

Bible stories abound with testimonies of answered prayer that you can share with children. When Daniel landed in the lion's den, he prayed for God's protection, and God answered his prayers. What a moment that must have been for Daniel and for the king. When you tell this story, emphasize to the kids that the God who heard Daniel's prayer hears our prayers today.

When we emphasize the power of prayer we reinforce to kids that God exists. They sense His presence, they see His answers to prayer, and they feel His love. We must also teach kids that prayer is not a wish list to a "heavenly Santa Claus," but is interactive communication between them and their heavenly Father. Prayer becomes a time of worship, relationship, and intercession, a strategic goal of their spiritual development

One Sunday school teacher told me of a boy in her class who grew up, got married, and had a baby born prematurely. The doctors didn't expect the baby to survive. This teacher had continued a friendship with this young man as he had grown. When she heard about the premature birth a week later, she called him and apologized for not being there to pray with him and his wife at the hospital. Joshua responded, "It's okay, Miss Judy. You weren't here to pray with us, but you taught me to pray when I was just a small boy. God has answered our prayers, and our baby is going to be fine." This story demonstrates the power of relationship and prayer. A child's Sunday school teacher still had a vital relationship in his life as a young man. The skills of prayer he learned as a small boy sustained him in an hour of desperate need over fifteen years later. When we teach children to pray, we impact their lives forever.

A vital goal for all who work in kids' ministry must be to teach kids to pray, to help them establish a close connection with God, who hears, cares, and answers. Prayer acts as a deep footer in the bedrock of a child's spiritual being, holding him or her fast in years to come. The goal for kids to be *powerful in prayer* is a first and strategic step in developing kids who will be strong enough to stand firm in Christ no matter what challenges come into their lives. Prayer builds spiritual champions.

Tips for Parents

Your kids need to hear you pray. Your prayers are an opportunity for the kids to discover that God exists. You naturally want to guard your kids against anxiety, yet it does them good to hear you pray about the difficulties you face. When you pray for your finances, or problems at work, or other needs, your kids learn that God can make a difference. When kids join you in prayer, they also get to join in the victory when that prayer is answered. Through prayer, they know that God is powerful. They know that God is good. They know that prayer works. They know that Christianity is real. These are the things that will sustain them through life.

Involve your kids in your daily life through prayer. Let them help pray through the trials and celebrate the answers. You can be sure they will face trials in their lives so give them a solid foundation of prayer to stand on. Even when God seems to say "no" to your prayers, you can help them understand that God doesn't always give us what we ask for, but He does give us what is best for us. When you learn how the thing you asked for would not have been good for you, share that with your kids as well. When that job you desperately wanted and didn't get ended up being terminated, share this provision with your kids. Let them discover how daily faith is lived out through trusting God in prayer. Teach them that God always answers prayer. Sometimes He says yes, sometimes He says no, and sometimes He says wait.

Tips for Kids Ministry Leaders

Give prayer time a prominent spot in your weekly sessions. The more kids participate in prayer, the more natural it will be for them to pray. Let them pray for one another's needs. Set aside time so they can pray at the altar. Teach them that prayer is not just asking for God's help but praising and thanking Him for Who He is and what He has done for us. Our job is to teach kids to pray. God's job is to answer their prayers and show them who He is—a faithful, powerful, and loving father, friend, and Lord. Never neglect an opportunity to help kids become powerful in prayer.

CHAPTER SEVEN

RESPONSIVE IN WORSHIP

The second goal for building resilient Christian kids is to teach them to be *responsive in worship*. Worship is the act of thanking God for His goodness and greatness. Worship lavishes love on the One who first loved us. Like prayer, worship introduces kids to a deeper understanding of God through intimate times with Him.[15] It fuels one's soul and nurtures one's relationship with God.[16] These divine moments with God sink spiritual roots deep into the soil of a child's life as they discover intimacy with God—unrehearsed, unmatched, and indescribable.

The spiritual journey of kids intensifies when they discover the joy of loving God. He wants kids to praise Him, for Scripture states, "Young men and women, old men and children. Let them praise the name of the LORD" (Ps. 148:12–13). The words "let them" convey a command from God. The writer could have used a term that would mean to "teach" them to praise the name of the Lord, but He used the stronger imperative form that indicates a command. God is serious about praise; as kids praise Him, they will know Him as a mighty and powerful God.

When I was a young child, I remember seeing people lift their hands and praise the Lord. I could see that their worship was genuine and meaningful to them. I could see that they truly loved God. For over a year I prayed, "God teach me to really love You!" I didn't realize it, but I was asking the God I had learned about to become the God I loved. I wish I could tell you how it happened or when it happened. But I do remember one day saying "Wow! I really do love God. He has answered my prayers!" I felt like the Psalmist who wrote, "Open my lips, LORD, and my mouth will declare your praise" (Ps. 51:15). God had opened my lips, and now I could praise Him and love Him and feel His love in return.

Teaching kids to love a God they can't see is a challenge, but God created them to desire a spiritual relationship with Him. As KidMin leaders invested their lives in me and gave me opportunity to pray and adore God, an intimate connection with Him grew in my young life. Their joy of worshipping God became my own.

During times of worship, kids discover a more intimate relationship with God than what they experience through prayer. As they show love and appreciation to God, He pours out His love and His presence on their young lives. Kids will cry while they worship God because their emotions are overwhelmed by His presence.

> DURING TIMES OF WORSHIP, KIDS DISCOVER A MORE INTIMATE RELATIONSHIP WITH GOD THAN WHAT THEY EXPERIENCE THROUGH PRAYER.

These intimate times of worship change kids' lives. Even "difficult" kids, as James Dobson writes, "are affected through time spent praising and worshiping God—for the presence of God influences our innermost being."[17] "Praise the LORD, my soul; all my inmost being, praise his holy name" (Ps. 103:1).

In kids' church, there are four significant opportunities for kids to be *responsive in worship*: during the song service, during an interlude segment, during the altar call, and during a prolonged altar experience. Leaders who want to instruct kids in worship will utilize these opportunities regularly. (While some of these activities are best suited for kids church, some are also appropriate in the classroom setting.)

THE SONG SERVICE

Worship involves more than songs that are typically sung in a church service.[18] It's quite possible to have a song service where little worship takes place. True worship involves heart-to-heart, loving communication between the individual and God. The heart is at the

> **WHEN WE TEACH KIDS TO WORSHIP GOD, WE MUST ALSO TEACH THEM TO LISTEN TO GOD.**

center of one's spiritual life. True worship occurs only when one sings or talks *to* God, not just *about* Him or His accomplishments. Often in kid's settings, songs sung to God include actions such as choreographed movements, clapping, etc. These portions of song services are fun, valuable, and usually introduce kids to concepts about God. However, true worship usually takes place when there are no distractions and children can center their thoughts fully on God.

Well-constructed song services include simple love songs to God. Outward signs of worship might include closed eyes, raised hands, heads pointed toward heaven or bowed in reverence, and lips moving in communication with God. These signs are clearly shown in Scripture, "I will praise you as long as I live, and in your name I will lift up my hands" (Ps. 63:4). Seeing kids fully engaged in worship for God is truly unmistakable. Kids hunger for these types of experiences. They are open and willing to be taught and influenced by individuals who love and worship God fervently.

Although kids have a natural hunger for God, they need simple training on how to love Him. Phrases such as, "Thank you, Jesus, for washing my sins away," "God, you are so good," and "I love you, Lord," provide kids with understandable terms to worship God. Kids are like dry kindling ready to be lit. Given the right encouragement and the right atmosphere and songs of worship, their young lives will be ignited to worship God, not only as children but throughout their entire lives. Great songs for worship contain short, easy-to-recall phrases that speak words of worship to God. These might include, "I love you, Lord," "I worship you, God," "You're so good." Once taught, these words will flow from a heart of thanksgiving as an offering of love.

When we teach kids to worship God, we must also teach them to listen to God. They need to know that God wants to speak to them on a daily basis. He will speak words of encouragement or instruction. Encourage kids to ask God to speak to them and to wait upon Him to speak. When we teach our kids to listen to the voice of God as they worship Him, we are preparing them to be spirit-led and spirit-empowered men and women.

INTERLUDES

Interludes are intervals within services or classroom teaching settings that provide an opportunity for kids to speak words of praise to God. Let's call these "power praise breaks." Typically, power praise breaks are between thirty seconds and three minutes. These interludes of worship teach kids that they can stop and thank God at any time when they remember great things He has done.[19] King David emphasized this when he proclaimed, "I will extol the LORD at all times; his praise will always be on my lips" (Ps. 34:1). Andy Park calls these private interludes with God, "climbing into the Father's lap."[20] He is right. The heavenly Father is constantly waiting for His children to climb into His lap, to show affection to the One who loves them.

ALTAR CALLS

Jorge knelt on the wooden gym floor at the front of kids' church. After a class on the importance of letting God's Spirit speak to us and tell us if what we're doing pleases Him or not, we invited all of the kids forward to spend time talking and listening to God. Although Jorge came alone to church on the church bus, he had been coming faithfully for some time. He had accepted Jesus and was learning how to live for God after years of negative influences in his home.

As Jorge knelt at the altar, a bit off by himself, he closed his eyes intently. Down each cheek rolled a tear. As I saw God moving on his life, I said to him, "You can feel God's presence, can't you, Jorge?" He nodded up and down—keeping his eyes tightly shut. "God is speaking to you right now, isn't He, Jorge?" I said. Again he nodded slowly. "You listen, and tell me later what He said, okay, Jorge?" This time Jorge didn't nod as he slipped deeper into a powerful encounter with the Spirit of God.

These divine moments around the altar at the front of your classroom or kids church can happen if you give God a chance and give Him the time. Many ministry leaders view the altar call only as an opportunity for a salvation response. However, time set aside at the altar in kids' classrooms and services is a prime opportunity for them to be still in God's presence and to worship Him. Kids can kneel at the front of an auditorium or at their seats. Whatever the physical setting, the place of worship needs to be a place of diminished distractions where kids can focus on God. This lets them respond to the message and spend time worshipping God. As kids learn to take time to worship God and hear His voice, their relationship with Him will deepen. The psalmist said, "I will praise you, LORD my God, with all my heart; I will glorify your name forever" (Ps. 86:12).

That's our goal: for kids to learn to worship God forever. We want them to get so hooked on being in the presence of God and loving Him that they never turn their backs on their relationship with Him.

PROLONGED ALTAR TIMES

During camp settings and special services for kids, prolonged times of praising, worshiping, and adoring God around the altar serve as life-changing experiences. During these occasions, kids hear special instructions from God regarding calls to ministry, to missionary service, to holiness, etc.[21] The more they experience God and learn to know Him, the more they will hunger for Him.

Spontaneous moves of God seem to occur at the leading of the Spirit of God during times of prayer and worship. Leaders who want to change kids' lives significantly will endeavor to provide these opportunities for their kids. When given the opportunity, kids bask in the sunshine of God's presence and are never the same,[22] for God has ordained it.

Kids respond to opportunities to worship God; however, we want to note two cautions. First, guard against using songs with words that are too complex for children to understand easily. When kids sing words they don't understand, they can become bored. No heart-to-heart communication takes place between a child and God when the child struggles with the meaning of the words.

A second caution is to avoid too much filler in your kids' services. The trend in some circles is to fill kids' services with so much fun and filler that little time is left for intimate and quiet times with God. One author, who described a "carnival" style of kids' services, stated, "Much of what takes place closely resembles entertainment in the culture at large, which may make it difficult for kids to experience awe and wonder before the majesty and holiness of God."[23] Granted, kids are drawn by fun and excitement, and kids' services must have an element of fun. However, kids are changed by a true relationship with the living God as discovered through intimate times with Him. One child who moved to a new town and attended a kids' service that was full of fun and filler stated, "I miss God." This child was missing the intimate moments with God she had experienced in her previous church. To the child, the service had become empty.

WORSHIP IN THE HOME

We have discussed the place of worship in a child's experiences at church; now let's discuss how children can experience worship in the home. As we stated previously, a parent is usually the gauge that sets the tone for the spiritual experience in the home. Most homes wouldn't have the same type of worship experiences as those at church, but there are several ways parents can include times of worship in their homes through music, thanksgiving sessions, and altar times. Parents who are responsive to God through worship in the home show kids the importance and value of a deep relationship with God.

People are moved by music. It has a way of grabbing our spirits and pointing us in one direction or another. Parents who provide godly Christian music in their homes are helping to establish a habit of worship in the lives of their kids. As kids hear songs about the greatness of God and His worthiness to receive praise, they naturally join in. Depending upon their age, they may or may not grasp the full meaning of a song, but as they do, they can truly worship God. Consider helping your child by introducing a song or explaining a song. The dialog might go like this. "I love this song. It's simple. I love singing it and inviting God to be here with me, guiding me every day."

When you introduce a song to your kids, you give them the opportunity not only to understand the meaning of the song but to understand what this song means to you and could mean to them.

You can plan to have a time of thanksgiving at the end of prayer times or when your family has received some good news. A parent might say, "Wow, God has healed grandma. The doctors say the lump is gone. They can't find it anywhere! Remember when we prayed about this? Let's take a moment and thank God for answering our prayer. He is such a good God."

Can you see how a power praise break can help your child learn to worship God? When you point out the great things God does for your family, you help your children associate giving thanks to God with expressing love for God.

When you spend time kneeling with your kids before bedtime, spend time not only in prayer but in worship. Be intentional in teaching your kids to worship God by sharing your love for God. Kids become *responsive in worship* when you show them how you enjoy spending quiet time with God. They can be open to God and enjoy a deep relationship with Him. They can sense His presence and hear His voice. Intimacy with God is a powerful force. Whether as a parent or as KidMin leader, I hope it will be your goal to take kids "back to the heart of worship, where it's all about you, it's all about you, Jesus."[24]

Kids who are *powerful in prayer* and *responsive in worship* are more likely to develop a deep and abiding relationship with God. They hear Him speak to them and they feel His presence. This creates an intimate relationship with God that will give them lasting spiritual strength.

Tips for Parents

Let your kids know how deeply you love God. Let them hear you worship Him. Let them see you lift your hands toward heaven and see tears of joy on your face. When they sense your closeness to Him, they will fall in love with the God you love.

Tips for Kids Ministry Leaders

What a joy it is when you lead a child into the presence of God and invite them to experience His presence through worship. What a thrill it is when you see them express their love to God, and you realize their relationship has deepened extensively and has become a conduit of love between them and God for the years ahead.

CHAPTER EIGHT

BIBLICALLY FLUENT

The workers came to King Josiah with amazing news. While remodeling the temple, they had found copies of the lost Scriptures (book of the law). In the fifty plus years of reign by his father and grandfather, these Scriptures had been lost or destroyed. Perhaps faithful priests of the past had intentionally hidden them for a day when a godly king might desire to read God's Word (see 2 Kings 22).

The third goal in developing kids who are firm believers is to help them become *biblically fluent*. We must teach kids to know God's Word (its values and judgments) and apply those values in everyday life. Biblical instruction introduces kids to the plans, promises, and commands of God. The Bible serves as a great reservoir of wisdom. By placing godly values deep in the hearts of children, it provides a blueprint for decisions they will make throughout their lives.

Mention teaching the Bible to kids, and unpleasant images may come to mind. You may think of a teacher, nose planted in a Sunday school quarterly, droning on and on while kids shoot spit wads and completely ignore her. Or you might think of a leader in kids' church who expounds eloquently on biblical subjects far beyond the understanding of children, while kids yawn in boredom or make faces at each other. You might think of parents who struggle to teach their kids the Word of God, so they avoid making any effort at all.

These examples represent well-meaning individuals who are inadequately trained in ministry to kids. When kids have to endure this type of teaching, they may grow to be teens or adults who are bored with

Christianity. But Bible teaching doesn't have to be boring if it's presented creatively. Picture a teacher standing on a chair—broom handle held high, pretending to be Goliath. The teacher has the attention of every kid in the room, and she asks pertinent questions like, "What did David feel like when he stood up in front of Goliath?" "He was scared," replies one child. "No, he wasn't," says another. "He'd already killed a bear and a lion."

This teacher understands the goal of helping kids become *biblically fluent*. She believes that God's Word reveals the character of God and can guide kids to depend on Him as their hero. Whether you're a teacher, KidMin leader, or parent, the steps to help kids become *biblically fluent* remain the same: (1) Provide biblical principles on a child's level of understanding; (2) provide opportunities for the child to experience God through the Bible lesson; (3) allow kids time to digest the biblical instructions and respond with questions; (4) apply the Bible truths to everyday life; (5) present the hope of the promises in God's Word; and (6) exemplify personal passion for this instructional letter from God—the Bible.

A CHILD'S LEVEL OF UNDERSTANDING

We must teach kids the principles of God's Word on the level they can comprehend. What kids can't comprehend, they can' learn. What they can't understand, can't change their lives. Capable KidMin leaders utilize language, concepts, and phrases on the child's level of understanding. This doesn't mean leaders avoid presenting difficult scriptural principles; rather, they use child-friendly concepts to convey deeper meanings.

Kids are the legacy and heritage of the church. Parents and KidMin leaders must invest time and energy to minister to them on their own level. Kids have the right to hear the Word of God in a way they can comprehend. Many parents and volunteers have good teaching skills, however, both parents and leaders must strive to communicate as creatively as possible in order to obtain long-lasting spiritual fruit.

> **KIDS HAVE THE RIGHT TO HEAR THE WORD OF GOD IN A WAY THEY CAN COMPREHEND.**

Tips for Parents

Many parents feel lost when it comes to passing Bible knowledge on to their kids. A great secret is to build on every gospel nugget that enters your life and your kids' lives. For example, after church you might set aside fifteen minutes in the car or at a restaurant or in a quiet outdoor setting to talk to your child about what they learned in Sunday school or kids' church. Ask about the Bible story, then quiz them on ways they can apply the lessons in the story to everyday life.

Another suggestion is to purchase a simple Bible story book that includes the main stories of the Bible. Work your way through it together. Read a story and take time to talk about the decisions of each character. Let your child describe what the characters were thinking and feeling and explain the spiritual value of those thoughts and feelings. Point out negative and positive consequences.

A third suggestion is to use products like Bible Fact-Pak Question Cards (purchased at www.MyHealthyChurch.com) for discussions with your kids. Use the questions as a game to see if mom or dad knows the answer or if the kids know the answer. Through the process, discuss the questions and answers.

Finally, look for an age-appropriate workbook at your local Bible bookstore or online. You can find excellent resources that have open-ended questions for kids to answer about a variety of subjects. For instance, a lesson about Samuel hearing the voice of God might ask, "Has God ever talked to you and given you instructions? Take the next week and listen for three instructions from God to you. Write them in your workbook." A workbook like this helps parents join in with the kids as they study various portions of Scripture. It provides excellent questions for parents to ask their kids that will stretch their faith and connect biblical instruction with everyday life.

Tips for Kids Ministry Leaders

KidMin leaders often have the advantage of a good curriculum; that is, if someone has taken time to make sure the publisher presents God as the author and the hero of our lives and presents a full scope and sequence of Bible doctrine. With that said, even the best curriculum won't have maximum impact unless the leader takes time to prepare and ask the Spirit of God to anoint the lesson. If you are a KidMin leader, consider reading your next Sunday's lesson on the previous Sunday afternoon. This gives God an entire week to speak to you about the lesson. Being Spirit-led means you give God time to tweak the lesson and make it more adaptable to the kids in your church. God will bring just the right illustration or object lesson to your mind to enhance the story. When a class is boring and the material is over the child's head, it often means the teacher didn't bother to prepare until the last minute.

EXPERIENCING GOD THROUGH THE BIBLE LESSON

Child-development specialists categorize learning styles as inborn traits and preferences that determine how children process information. A kid will learn best when the teacher uses that kid's particular style of learning to present the lesson. Effective KidMin leaders use variety and creativity when they communicate with kids. Three of the most prevalent learning styles are visual, auditory, and kinesthetic.

The *visual learner* craves lessons filled with action, pictures, props, DVDs, and other visual elements. This child's interest is pricked by visual stimuli and the anticipation of something new. A visual child will imagine Goliath's ugly face, scowling in hatred. When visual learners can see someone standing in Goliath's shoes, they lock the image of that moment in their minds. Tied to these images is the lesson portrayed— David was afraid when he stood before Goliath, yet he believed and trusted God. David went forward, took aim with his sling shot, and God provided a miracle. David was rewarded for being brave, but the child learns that God our hero provided the miracle!

Auditory learners listen intently. These kids hear every voice inflection and every detail of the story. They can mimic the voice of Goliath just like their teacher. They seem intuitively to know answers to questions since they haven't missed a word. When teachers tell Bible stories with vitality and creativity, these learners imbed the power of God's miraculous workings deep into their memories.

The *kinesthetic learner* must be active to learn. When the teacher acts like young David standing before Goliath, uttering his harsh sacrilege, this child experiences the emotions and expectations that David must have felt. The kinesthetic learner hungers to be a part of the action. Action evokes emotion, which creates great learning opportunities for this child.

Wise teachers vary presentations with a mixture of methods to appeal to kids' different learning styles. Creative parents will also use a variety of methods to make Bible lessons come to life. Leaders must always strive to grow in their teaching abilities; this includes making use of the latest gadgets and teaching tools. You can be sure that the kids are probably well aware of the latest resources even before the teacher. There's no lack of valuable resources to help present exciting and meaningful lessons. These might include: DVDs, object lessons, skits, puppetry, crafts, drama, human video, storytelling, illusions, balloon animals, games, and shadow art, just to name a few. Great KidMin leaders and parents never stop learning new techniques for presenting lessons in ways that will plant God's Words in kid's minds and instill spiritual values in their lives.

Tips for Parents

The various learning styles may seem daunting, but keep in mind that no KidMin leader knows your child as well as you do. You have the advantage of knowing how your child likes to learn. You also have the opportunity to teach one-on-one or in a relatively small group. Kids who get to talk, ask questions, and explore the story with you are usually applying their learning styles in the process.

Don't be afraid to act silly. Walk and talk like Goliath. Whirl an imaginary sling shot around your head like David. Encourage your kids to act out Bible stories. Let them be the lions Daniel faced. Read the story fresh for yourself. Don't just tell it from memory. When most adults reread a Bible story they discover a truth or fact they had missed before. This may be the Holy Spirit leading you towards a particular slant of the story.

Ask your kids questions about the stories of the Bible. This is a great way to discover where they are at spiritually. It may surprise you. Ask your kids if the Holy Spirit is saying anything to them. Again you'll be surprised at the amazing lessons the Holy Spirit may be teaching your child. Answer something like, "Wow, you really did hear from the Holy Spirit, didn't you?" This affirms what they have heard and makes them want to hear more.

Tips for Kids Ministry Leaders

Don't feel inadequate if these learning styles are new to you. Most good curriculums include segments designed to meet the various learning styles. Take time to watch your kids as they play and interact with each other. Learn what seems to connect with them and what doesn't. Ask your kids what they remembered from the week before. Usually they'll recall details from the portion of the class that connected with them the most. It will be a clue to what really impacted them.

Invite guests into your classroom for a cameo appearance; they can provide a unique slant on a story or lesson. A new person is always interesting and automatically connects with kids in new ways.

Make sure to emphasize God in each part of the story. It was God who rescued Shadrach, Meshach, and Abednego. It was God who rescued Joseph from prison. It was God who divided the Red Sea. The kids need to see God as their faithful, powerful provider: their hero.

DIGEST AND RESPONSE

Helping kids become *biblically fluent* isn't about rote memory but about creating permanent values. It's not enough to know the words of the Bible; kids must comprehend the truths behind the words in order

KIDS' QUESTIONS BEGIN DEEP WITHIN THEIR SPIRITS AND SEEM TO OPEN WIDE A DOOR INSIDE.

to integrate the values of the Bible. When kids learn about the values of biblical figures they incorporate those principles into their own lives. When kids discover that David was afraid when he stood before Goliath, yet he acted in faith because he trusted in God, this produces faith in their young hearts. Through this process they develop a biblical morality and spiritual faith that will guide them throughout life.

Do you ever wonder where you heard various Bible stories for the first time? Do you ever wonder where your faith in God began? How it became strong? Why it lasted? Purposely infusing kids' lives with Bible instruction is a process that builds spiritual strength and fortitude in their hearts.

As kids digest Bible lessons, their minds develop questions. Good communicators provide opportunities for questions and respond in sincerity. Kids' questions begin deep within their spirits and seem to open wide a door inside. Once they ask a question, there's a moment when they and all the kids wait expectantly for the response. In that moment the deep recesses of their spirits are open for deposit.

When we ask kids what Daniel felt in the lion's den or what Jesus felt on the cross, the child experiences the emotion of that moment. This elicits an internal response as they understand that Daniel determined to do what was right, regardless of his fear—or that Jesus loved us enough to die on the cross. Emotions create a lasting link to children's hearts.[25] Emotions draw the principles of the story down deep. Emotions take God the hero deep into the spirit of the child as they see God act in amazing ways and determine He can act on their behalf as well.

Kids' questions provide glimpses into their minds. A child who asks if God is mean very possibly doesn't have an experience with a loving father. A child who asks if cheating is wrong may very well be feeling guilty for cheating. Questions allow parents and leaders to adapt the lesson to the open soil of the kid's mind.

There are times when questions may be a tangent that is off the course of the lesson. However, Spirit-led KidMin leaders or parents will recognize a tangent as an opportunity to cover a topic of significant interest to the kids. This reminds me of an experience I heard recently from a friend of mind.

One Sunday morning the curriculum for the fourth grade class was about John the Baptist. The teacher was acting out the angel speaking to John's father, explaining to John that his baby boy would be someone special, and that his name would be John. Suddenly, a hand shot up? "God already knew his name?" one child asked? "Yes," the teacher replied. "So, God really knows all about the baby before it's born?" the child added. "Yes, of course," answered the teacher.

Not sure where these questions were going but sensing the interest of the child and the rest of the class, the teacher added, "The Bible says that God knows our names before we are even born." Contemplating this, another child blurted out, "So abortion really is wrong then? The baby is a real person with a name and everything. It would be like killing the baby person." A hush fell over the room as the teacher saw the turn in the topic of the morning.

Being an astute teacher, she stopped and said "Yes, abortion is killing a real live baby that God created. He knows the baby's name and everything about the baby. Would you like to talk about abortion a little bit?" Hands shot up around the room. "My aunt had an abortion," one child said. "My sister's pregnant," said another. "Killing a baby is wrong isn't it?" a third child asked.

The teacher allowed the kids not only to ask questions but to decide some of the answers. Kids said things like, "Of course it's wrong. The baby had a name." The teacher then turned to the passage in Psalms 139:16 and read, "Your eyes saw my unformed body; all the days ordained for me were written in your book before one of them came to be." And Psalms 139:13, "You knit me together in my mother's womb" The teacher explained that not only does God know each person's name while they are still in their mother's body, He knows everything about their life and what He created them to do. Some people will be doctors, teachers, pastors, or KidMin leaders. God doesn't want babies to be killed because He has a plan for each person's life.

That day it seemed like God wanted the class to receive insight for their spiritual development that included "unborn babies are real people." This happened because the teacher recognized a wild tangent for a spirit-led moment—and the tangent occurred because the teacher stopped, allowed questions, and gave the kids a chance to digest and respond to the discussion.

Time to digest and respond lets kids discover the key points of the lesson you intended to teach or the lesson the Holy Spirit intended you to teach. It can all happen through a question that grabs the attention of the whole class. Kids need time to digest and respond to the lesson, and questions help this process. Frequently, their questions are deeper than one might imagine because they comprehend far more than we think and the Spirit of God is at work in their lives—enhancing the biblical comprehension. A discerning teacher can glean valuable information about a child through the questions he asks and the responses he gives.

Here are a few guidelines regarding questions:

1. Ask questions to all.
2. Discuss questions as kids provide them.
3. Ask follow-up questions.
4. Don't be afraid of silence. Kids are thinking.
5. Use open-ended questions, not yes and no questions.
6. Ask questions that involve feelings, decisions, or choices.
7. Ask questions about God's involvement in the story.

Tips for Parents

Don't be afraid of questions. When you don't know the answer to a question, say so. Explain that you'll try to find an answer, or direct the child to ask someone who would know the answer: "That would be a good question for your teacher." When kids ask questions, their minds are open to be influenced by scriptural principles. It would be better to spend several weeks on one Bible story or concept due to lots of questions, than to skim through Bible stories without really learning what they are saying to us today.

Tips for Kids Ministry Leaders

One of the gravest mistakes leaders make is when they do all the talking. Kids learn by participating in the class; they learn by talking. Let them explore the scriptural text. Don't give them all the answers. When the class is split over the answer to a question, give them time to discuss why they feel the way they do. Each story in the Bible has dozens of nuggets of spiritual truths waiting to be discovered.

When younger kids are coloring pictures, making Noah's ark animals out of Playdough, or building the fiery furnace out of blocks, that's a great time to ask them questions about the story. Their hands are busy; let their minds be busy as well. Kids say amazing things about God while their hands are busy and their spirit is free to be engaged by the Holy Spirit.

EVERYDAY LIFE

"What did you learn in church today?" asked Mom. "Oh, it was about some airplane guy who said Jesus had to die," replied Henry. "I'm not sure I understand," Mom said. "Wasn't your class about Good Friday or Easter or something like that?" "I suppose it was," Henry agreed. "This airplane pilot said Jesus had to die, but the Barabby guy got to go free." "Are you talking about Pontius Pilate and Barabbas? Pilate wasn't an airline pilot; that was his last name."

I like how the mother in this humorous illustration took advantage of the opportunity to correct her son's understanding of a Bible story.

An everyday application like this can mean the difference between learning and living. When kids hear the story of David and Goliath, they need to apply the lesson to their own lives. That's how they learn God's principles for life. Sometimes applications impact kids powerfully, creating "divine moments" with God. That's what happened in the story we shared earlier about abortion. The Holy Spirit took the lesson and created a powerful moment that gave those kids a biblical "takeaway" for their everyday lives.

Most of the curriculum for kid includes segments of practical application. Leaders should emphasize the relevance of these lessons to help kids apply them to everyday life. Questions can help with this process. Ask kids what the lesson means to them. Ask why the Bible character did what they did. Even the stories of sinful individuals in the Bible have lessons for us to learn. Don't be too quick to provide the answers. As kids contemplate practical application, they learn.

Discussion groups are also an excellent way to convey practical application. Kids love to talk. When you encourage them to discuss the lesson of the day in small groups you engage their minds, which establishes both learning and relevancy. For instance, some lessons you might discuss from the story of David and Goliath include: faith in God's provision, obedience to one's superiors, the value of hard work, courage in the midst of difficult times, God's mighty power, and many more. Kids who discover new principles feel as if they have dug out their own personal nugget from the pages of Scripture. These nuggets form a strong foundation that will hold them solid in the years ahead, because they are Spirit-led discoveries. The Holy Spirit is the best teacher. Times of questions and discussion give kids time to think and gives the Holy Spirit the opportunity to speak. These kids are becoming *biblically fluent*!

DVD's are a great tool for parents who need something creative and yet simple to present. However, instead of merely watching the video, stop it every five minutes or so and take time to ask questions. Talk about situations in everyday life that might be similar to the situations in the Bible story. This helps the child to tie everyday lessons to the biblical account.

In his research, George Barna found that many teenagers grew up in church learning biblical principles but failed to apply those principles to everyday life.[26] It is vitally important that kids learn both biblical facts and practical application for daily life. We must teach them to apply the lessons to their own lives. This is a key to a lifelong relationship with God: to learn that the Holy Spirit will take the lessons of the Bible and speak to us and show us how to apply them to our lives. Application is the goal of teaching. It builds strength for a child's spiritual future.

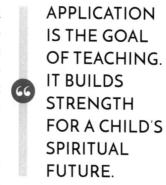

APPLICATION IS THE GOAL OF TEACHING. IT BUILDS STRENGTH FOR A CHILD'S SPIRITUAL FUTURE.

Tips for Parents

Strive for biblical application in everyday life. When daily circumstances happen, use previous Bible lessons to show biblical application. If something unfortunate happens, recall the story of Daniel being taken away as a slave. God still had a plan and purpose for his life. God used him in great ways. God will guard and guide your family as well.

As mentioned previously, talk about the child's lesson on the way home from church. See if your child has found the link between the Bible lesson and everyday life. The story might have been about Joseph, but the child may have come away with thoughts like:

> *Wow, Joseph forgave his brothers.*
> *Wow, I don't want to be mean to my brother any more.*
> *Wow, Joseph had step brothers, and he loved them.*
> *Wow, Joseph's dad really missed him.*
> *Wow, Joseph had to live in prison? I guess our mobile home isn't so bad.*

STRONG ENOUGH TO LAST

> **KIDS WHO LEARN THE JOY OF DIGGING INTO GOD'S WORD ARE KIDS WHO WILL DELIGHT IN GOD'S WORD FOREVER.**

All of these and many more are potential lessons the Holy Spirit may have deposited in the heart of your child from one Bible story.

Tips for Kids Ministry Leaders

Don't forget to ask your kids about things that happened to them during the previous week. Often something that happened in the lives of your students or their families ties in with the Bible stories you have been studying. Tie together the daily circumstances that affect us all and the guidance we find in the Bible that helps us live victoriously through such circumstances.

Don't forget to ask the kids for the answers before you give them. Your conversation might go as follows:

"So your best friend got mad at you and said mean things about you on the playground, Delaya?" the teacher asked.

"Yes, and I'm not gonna talk to her anymore," Delaya replied.

The teacher looked around the classroom. "Class, we've been studying the story of Joseph the last few weeks, haven't we? What have we learned?"

After a long pause, Jayden said, "Not to be like Joseph's brothers and beat people up."

Andrew chimed in, "Or do mean things like hating each other."

Lynelle said, "But we're still supposed to forgive them like Joseph did."

Delaya said, "But I don't want to forgive my friend. She hurt me."

The teacher responded, "Do you think Joseph was hurt too? They hurt him, took his coat, ripped it up, and then sold him as a slave."

Lynelle turned in her chair and said, "I think you should forgive her, Delaya. I will go with you."

A smile spread across Delaya's face. "I suppose you're right. It was my fault anyway. I spilled juice on her new shoes."

A conversation like this takes last week's lesson and brings it home to everyday life. Don't worry if discussions like these dip into the time you scheduled for the class. Let the Holy Spirit guide your teaching!

BIBLICAL PROMISES

The wonderful promises in God's Word provide kids with hope, joy, and faith. Promises fulfilled through answers to prayer greatly enhance the expectation of further promises. The God who heals is the same God who promises eternal life in heaven. These promises grow kids' faith. Individuals who emphasize not only the moral principles in God's Word, but also the vast array of promises recorded in Scripture, instill a joyful hope in kids' lives.

Throughout the Bible we find promises are both recorded and implied. Learning to search for God's promises serves as a great lifelong habit for kids. Fortunately, there are many tools that list the promises of God. Often, you can find such lists in the back of a Bible. A great lesson is not only to ask kids weekly, "What has the Holy Spirit said to you this week?" but also to ask "What promises have you found in the Bible this week?" Kids who learn the joy of digging into God's Word are kids who will delight in God's Word forever.

Tips for Parents

Consider compiling a list of promises that you discover together as a family. What a spiritual treasure it would be to have dozens of promises recorded as a family. These promises will be there when the family needs to turn to them. Each child will have them as precious jewels for the years ahead—an inheritance of promises from God bestowed through a loving parent.

As well, be sure and take note when God's promises come true—such as when God provides a new house or a new job or new car. Make note when God heals or when He restores something that was taken.

Tips for Kids Ministry Leaders

What are your favorite promises? Do your kids know what they are and why? Have your kids heard the many times God was there to meet your needs and supply His blessings when it was needed most?

Consider creating a wall of promises in your kids' areas. As kids discover a new promise in the Bible at home, have them write it down on a piece of paper and bring it to church. When they do, reward them with a treat. Kids love rewards!

PERSONAL PASSION

Kids will love learning God's Word when they see leaders who love God's Word. When you show your passion for the Bible, you elevate its value in the eyes of the kids. When leaders go to the Bible for answers or quote the promises of Scripture, kids learn the importance of the Word of God. Your passion for God and His Word will translate into kids who love God because they see how much you love Him!

KidMin leaders and parents are both mentors, and the greatest way they mentor is by being a godly example and by having a loving relationship with the child. Kids will fall in love with what their mentors love. If mentors love to pray, kids will love to pray. If mentors love to worship, so will the kids. The same is true with the Word of God. Mentors build relationships with kids, and these relationships are powerful. Fortunately, God does His part. Remember the Holy Spirit is the greatest teacher. Mentors introduce kids to God, the Holy Spirit, and the Word of God through the example of their own lives.

Tips for Parents

Make every effort to let your kids see your love for God and His Word. They watch you very closely. They will learn to value what you value, and treasure what you treasure. Their lives are soft clay. Now is the time to impress godly teaching and application upon their spirits that will last a lifetime.

Tips for Kids Ministry Leaders

Be alert to each and every opportunity possible to show your love for God. This motivates kids to love Him, too, and to become champions—passionate for God.

The principles in God's Word take a lifetime to discover, yet the basics come quickly. Both parents and KidMin leaders must teach biblical values that will help children honor and serve God the rest of their lives. When we reach kids who don't have Christian parents, we bear an added responsibility for their spiritual development. But we must teach and guide all children so they will be guided by godly principles and promises for life. In this way we build spiritual strength and depth that will endure the storms of life.

If we're going to accomplish this enormous task, we need parents who will not only invest in the lives of their kids at home but will make sure they regularly attend multiple weekly services at church—including both large and small group models. This gives kids the maximum opportunity to bond with multiple spiritual leaders who can impact their lives in different ways.

Sometimes churches try to combine large- and small-group teaching applications into one mega service. While these applications may be the best a church can do under their circumstances, the large group setting rarely duplicates the quality of relationships that are built in small groups.[27] Multiple learning opportunities, such as Sunday school, kids' church services, and mid-week clubs take more effort, but they result in stronger spiritual foundations in kids due to repeated opportunities to learn biblical values. Unfortunately, many churches are de-emphasizing Sunday school classes and mid-week programs, often due to the inability to train and recruit workers.[28] We must move with care in this area, taking into consideration the responsibility of the church to provide spiritual training for future generations of kids. In other words, to help kids live for God the rest of their lives, we must give them the maximum opportunities possible to bond with leaders at church and with parents at home!

Can you imagine if we didn't have the Bible to read as it was in the day of Josiah? He had evidently known of the things of God through verbal instruction because there were no copies of the Word of God. When he found the Word of God, he was thrilled. When he read it, he was devastated at the true state of his heart, his people, and his nation. He repented on behalf of his nation. Our kids must know the Word of God and how it applies to their lives if they are to avoid the devastation sin brings.

CHAPTER NINE

SPIRIT EMPOWERED

Two years after I sat and prayed in the fork of the tree and heard God's voice, I attended a church that taught about being baptized in the Holy Spirit. I remember learning that the Holy Spirit was a free gift from God designed to help Christians live their lives for Christ. More than anything, I wanted that gift!

For over two weeks I sought the baptism in the Holy Spirit. I prayed at home, I prayed at church. Sometimes I prayed alone and sometimes other people prayed for me. I experienced such joy and peace during those times of prayer–feeling my relationship with God grow. Then one Sunday night when I prayed at the altar, I felt God move upon me in a powerful way, and I responded by speaking in words I couldn't understand. It was an amazingly joyous time! Instantly I knew I had been filled with the Holy Spirit just like the disciples. People around me also knew that I had been baptized in the Holy Spirit.

W hen kids are *Spirit empowered*, this enhances the depth of the three previous goals. If we let Him, the Holy Spirit will launch the learning experience into new and powerful realms. He imparts power—power for ministry, power for service, power for evangelism, and power to live for God forever.

This gift is of such significance that Jesus told His disciples to "wait for the gift My Father promised" (Acts 1:4). He said, "Stay in the city until you have been clothed with power from on high" (Luke 24:49). Jesus knew the days ahead would be difficult for His disciples. He knew they would endure great difficulties and would need the power of the Holy Spirit to remain faithful. Just as the disciples needed the power of the Holy Spirit, kids today need this power as well.

It isn't difficult to imagine the sorrow Peter felt after he denied Jesus and watched Him die on the cross. Then what joy he must have felt when God raised Christ from the dead. Jesus forgave Peter and spent time with him and the other disciples before ascending into heaven. During that time Jesus promised to send the Comforter to fill their lives with power. What excitement must have filled Peter's heart. Something was coming—Jesus had promised it!

The baptism of the Holy Spirit is a free gift from God, through Jesus, for all believers. John the Baptist described this gift when he stated, "He [Jesus] will baptize you with the Holy Spirit and fire" (Matt. 3:11). And Luke wrote that this promise is a gift for everyone, young and old. "The promise is for you and your children" (Acts 2:39). The gift of the Holy Spirit improves a child's ability to pray, praise, and comprehend God's Word. This empowerment makes the child bold to live for Jesus Christ. As mentioned previously, a large percentage of young people fail to continue in their relationship with Christ during their teenage years. These youth need to have God's power and godly resources available to them as early in their spiritual journey as possible in order to fortify them against the pressures and temptations of life. The baptism in the Holy Spirit is God's gift for this purpose. We must not neglect to teach our children about this powerful gift.

When the disciples were filled with the Holy Spirit, they spoke in tongues as an evidence that they had been filled (Acts 2:4). Throughout the book of Acts we see in the early church that as people were saved they also sought this free gift from God. One-by-one they were filled with the Holy Spirit and began to speak in tongues (Acts 8:14–17; 10:44–47; 19:1–7). This evidence of tongues not only was a sign to show that the person had received God's gift, it also served as a tool of prayer and praise—enhancing both.

Being *spiritually empowered* helps kids *respond in worship*. On the day of Pentecost, those in the upper room were filled with the Holy Spirit and began to speak in tongues (Acts 2:4). The people heard these disciples speaking words of praise to God. "We hear them declaring the wonders of God in our own tongues" (Acts 2:11). Obviously, one use of this prayer language is for the individual to worship God and declare the wonders He has done. Kids often run out of words to express their love to God. They don't know what to say. When they are filled with the Spirit, they can worship God in their prayer language and draw closer to Him.

> **THE ABILITY TO PRAY IN TONGUES IS COMFORTING FOR KIDS WHO OFTEN RUN OUT OF WORDS TO PRAY TO GOD.**

Speaking in tongues also helps kids be *powerful in prayer*. In certain situations, Christians don't know how to pray or what to pray for (Rom. 8:26). The ability to pray in tongues is comforting for kids who often run out of words to pray to God. As a kids' camp speaker for many years, I have watched thousands of kids intercede before God using the prayer language they received from Him. It's amazing to see the intimacy these kids exhibit in the presence of God. No longer do they run out of words to pray, instead they pray for hours.

As amazing as the evidence of speaking in tongues is for the Christian, it is the minor part of the gift of the Holy Spirit, which is a gift of power for service. Speaking in tongues is evidence of the gift and a tool to assist in communicating with God. The gift of the Holy Spirit also provides miraculous power and boldness to witness for Christ. *Spirit-empowered* kids receive this power and boldness. As they watch God do miraculous things in and through their lives, their faith grows. As they boldly stretch forth their hands to pray and see God use them in miraculous healings, this builds a powerful faith in God. This great gift of power and boldness increases the faith of kids and establishes them in a deep and lifelong faith.

The gift of the Holy Spirit also enhances a kid's ability to be *biblically fluent*. Jesus promised the disciples that when the Holy Spirit came upon

> **LIFE IS OFTEN DIFFICULT FOR KIDS, BUT THE COMFORT OF THE HOLY SPIRIT WILL HELP THEM ALL THEIR LIVES.**

them, He (the Holy Spirit) would teach them all things (John 14:26). When the disciples received this gift, they were changed remarkably. Moments after being filled with the Spirit, Peter (who had denied Christ earlier) stood up and preached and 3,000 people were saved. The difference in their lives was evident to all as they boldly spread the good news of Jesus. "Paul and Barnabas spent considerable time there, speaking boldly for the Lord, who confirmed the message of his grace by enabling them to perform signs and wonders" (Acts 14:3).

Kids need the power of the Holy Spirit. Jesus told the disciples the gift of the Holy Spirit was a gift of power to help them witness. "You will receive power when the Holy Spirit comes on you; and you will be my witnesses" (Acts 1:8). This gift of power will help our kids to witness to others. The Holy Spirit gives them courage and teaches them what to say.

Jesus called the Holy Spirit the Comforter. He told the disciples the Holy Spirit would come and help them. The Holy Spirit continues to serve as a Comforter for kids today. This promised gift is available to them. Life is often difficult for kids, but the comfort of the Holy Spirit will help them all their lives.

The night I was filled with the Holy Spirit, my younger sister was also filled. Later that night my youngest brother was instantly filled with the Spirit in my bedroom. My infilling was the inspiration for him to desire this gift. Today both my sister and brother are dedicated Christians who serve in their local churches. Many leaders and teachers influenced their young lives, but the power of the Holy Spirit in their lives helped them remain faithful to this day.

Kids need every advantage to grow in faith and in the knowledge of God and His Word if they are to serve Him faithfully throughout their lives. Jesus commanded the disciples to wait for this gift of power for He knew they needed it. Kids need it as well. Randy Christensen says, "Leaders who give their children opportunity to learn about this promised blessing from God give them the opportunity to enhance their ability to pray, praise, and grow in Jesus"[29]

The goal for kids to be *Spirit empowered* augments the effectiveness of the first three goals. By helping kids attain these four goals, we build and solidify their faith for today and for the future. We help to strengthen the formation of their spiritual being.

Tips for Parents

Often parents don't understand the baptism in the Holy Spirit and don't feel equipped to talk to their kids about it. The parents themselves may have questions about this experience. Here are a few points to understand in order to discuss this experience with your kids. The baptism in the Holy Spirit is a free gift God gives to Christians to help them live powerfully and boldly for Him. This gift doesn't save us or insure a spot in heaven. Rather, it equips us to stay the course by giving us power to serve God.

Everyone receives the baptism in the Holy Spirit through an encounter with God that usually begins with a desire to receive more from God. This great gift was given to the disciples as recorded in Acts chapter two and is being given to millions of Christians today. It begins with a simple prayer, asking God for this great blessing. Then, as each individual seeks, desires, and prays for more of God, whether it takes minutes, hours, days, or weeks, that person receives this great gift of God. The gift of speaking in tongues accompanies the baptism in the Holy Spirit as a clear sign that the person has been filled.

A friend of mine who was a Christian worker came to me one day and stated that he had always wanted to be filled with the Holy Spirit but had never had this experience. As we talked, I realized that he seemed to want it but didn't desire it with great fervor. I challenged him to ask God to be baptized in the Holy Spirit every day for a month. He called me on day nineteen with his new story of God's great power in his life.

Outdoors by a camp fire, all by himself, the power of God came upon him, and he was filled with the Spirit and began to speak in a brand new prayer language, which he uses to this day.

With kids this isn't the norm. When they want something they seem to want it badly! Therefore, when they are hungry for God, they tend to receive this infilling quickly! At age thirteen, I prayed for two weeks and received. My little brother prayed for ten minutes!

Tips for Kids Ministry Leaders
Kids need to know that God wants to give them the special gift of the baptism in the Holy Spirit. Share with them the biblical accounts of this experience. Teach the kids to pray, asking God for this great gift. Kids are often filled with the Holy Spirit in classrooms, services, altar times, and in their own bedrooms as they have a special encounter one-on-one with God.

Fortunately, God has made it very clear so you will never have to wonder if a child has received this gift or not. God isn't an author of confusion. God gave clear evidence that the disciples used and experienced. They knew someone had been filled when they heard that person speak in tongues. Even people they didn't think could be filled were filled, and the disciples heard them speak in tongues and praise God (Acts chapter 10). Remember, speaking in tongues is praying to God in a language we don't know. It can be an earthly language or a heavenly language (1 Cor. 14:2).

After kids have been baptized in the Holy Spirit, continue to teach them about the gifts of the Spirit and the power that occurred through the lives of the disciples and continues to occur today. Kids can be *Spirit empowered* and used through prayer, wisdom, knowledge, miracles, and much more.

I have often talked with believers who just aren't sure about this gift. Perhaps as a child they were taught it didn't exist. Years ago I taught a class of adults who had come to our church, but who had questions about this gift. They all agreed to pray, "God, if this is of you and it is real, we want it!" Over the course of about ten weeks, it was amazing to watch as these twenty or so adults were filled with the Holy Spirit. Not one of them was filled in class—they were all filled at home or at other places where they prayed. No one coerced them to have this experience. They simply prayed for more of God, and they wanted this gift if it truly was from Him. It happened! "Ask and it will be given to you; seek and you will find, knock and the door will be opened to you. . . . How much more will your Father in heaven give the Holy Spirit to those who ask him!" (Luke 11:9–13) God wants all believers to ask, seek, and knock for this great gift.

CHAPTER TEN

GIVING SELFLESSLY

"All I want for my birthday is Bibles," one eight-year-old boy in Louisiana announced. "There are people in Bosnia who don't have Bibles, and I want Bibles for my birthday so I can mail them to Bosnia."

W e're all selfish by nature, which means that *giving selflessly* is *not* a natural trait whether you're five years old or fifty. Isn't that why we have to teach our kids as early as toddlers not to hoard their toys but to share them with others? Today's media-driven society strives to convince our young people that life is "all about me." Expensive shoes, clothing, toys, and gadgets surround the average teen, and Christian kids are often swept into this same lifestyle.

Compassion is the biblical value that teaches us to care more about others than we do about ourselves. Interestingly, it seems that compassion can be taught and caught if it is emphasized while kids are still young. Kids can become individuals who *give selflessly.*

Teaching kids about the lost people of the world stirs something godly in their spirits. When they learn about the plight of underprivileged kids around the world, who live without shelter, clothing, food, or water, something stirs in their hearts and compassion is born. Kids begin to care at a young age. Caring is followed by praying. Praying is followed by *sacrificially giving,* and giving is followed by going.

Statistics show that many, many kids who were taught about missions not only developed a heart of compassion at a very young age, but continued on this missionary journey their whole lives. Not only did they become missionaries, they lived for God their entire lives. A heart filled with godly compassion became a steadfast anchor throughout their lives.

My wife, Mary, and I lead the kids' missions arm of our fellowship called Boys and Girls Missionary Challenge (BGMC). When children hear about the needs of people around the world, they learn to care about others. Once they care, they want to act. It's a God-given passion that resides within them—ready to be touched by the Spirit of God. This action is at the heart of Christian discipleship. When Jesus told the parable of the good Samaritan, He taught that the essence of a true believer is a willingness to act on behalf of the needy. All other religiosity is false. The priest and Levite in that story didn't act like Christ because they cared for themselves but not for the man on the road who desperately needed help. When a child chooses to pray for the lost, it is because the child has begun to care. Caring is at the heart of compassion. A child with a compassionate heart begins to see that life has value when it is spent serving others.

That's why *giving selflessly* is such an important goal to teach kids. When we teach them to care about the lost people of the world, the poor of the world, and the needy people in their own towns, we help them to understand that each of us has value in God's kingdom. We give them the opportunity to become like the good Samaritan.

The Louisiana boy in the introduction to this chapter did get Bibles for his birthday. In fact, he got more than eighty Bibles. But he didn't realize that the English Bibles he collected couldn't be read by the Bosnians, so the people in his church got involved. They donated the English Bibles to a good cause and purchased and shipped eighty Bosnian Bibles to be distributed in Bosnia. This boy chose to act selflessly. Rather than ask for something for himself on his birthday, he asked for gifts he could give to others. Compassion and the power of the Spirit were moving upon this young boy.

Today in the Assemblies of God, thousands and thousands of kids give over seven million dollars a year to help meet the needs of lost and needy people around the world. We hear about kids who sell their toys at garage

> ## AS KIDS SHARE THEIR TALENTS THEY BEGIN TO KNOW WHO THEY ARE AND HOW THEY CAN CONTRIBUTE TO THE KINGDOM OF GOD.

sales so they have more money to give. God speaks to their hearts, and they act. That's true discipleship—they put into practice what they have learned by listening to the voice of the Spirit. These kids have discovered God. They have learned to hear His voice, they have decided to obey His voice, and they have chosen to act upon what they heard. These kids are well on their way to being lifelong followers of Christ.

So often we hear of kids who are called to full-time Christian service after they have been involved in selfless giving. When they are immersed in praying for the lost of the world and *giving selflessly to* help the needy in their communities, their hearts are open to hear God say "Well done!" And they hear His call into full-time service.

When nine-year-old Michael collected Bibles for Bosnia, his heart was stirred with compassion. Because his heart was tender and open to the Spirit of God, he heard God say, "You are to go to Bosnia as a missionary, now. Not when you grow up; you are to go now." Michael was thrilled. He told his parents that God wanted them to become missionaries and move to Bosnia.

As you can imagine, his parents were quite shocked, but they had also heard a call from God to be missionaries. They just didn't know where. In the years ahead, this family did become missionaries to the country of Bosnia.

Kids hear the voice of God. Their compassionate hearts are ready to be filled with the Spirit of God. *Giving selflessly* is a vital step in developing deep and abiding faith in the heart of a child. As they give selflessly, kids will also want to *actively serve*. As kids share their talents they begin to know who they are and how they can contribute to the kingdom of God.

Tips for Parents

Decide that yours will be a generous home. Expose your kids to the needs of the poor and lost of the world. Not only will this expand their hearts to include others, it will give them a new awareness of how blessed they are and how thankful they should be. There are many books, DVDs, and other resources available to introduce your kids to the needs of the world. (Many resources are available at www.bgmc. ag.org) Your children need to realize that God loves the kids of the world just as much as He loves them. He knows each child by name and wants each one to know Him as Lord and Savior.

Tips for Kids Ministry Leaders

Don't neglect this important goal in your kid's lives. *Giving selflessly* is the opposite of greed and selfishness. We live in a world driven by greed. As kids get older, they will be inundated with worldly propaganda trying to convince them they deserve more and more stuff. They will be told that life is all about them and what they have.

Compassion insulates kids against this kind of greed. Once they compare their lives to those of others around the world, they will be happy with their own lives and will view themselves as a solution to the needs of others. A heart that is willing to *give selflessly* is a heart that will hold firmly to a deep faith in God.

Search for resources to teach your kids about the needs of the world. A great wealth of free resources are available at www.bgmc.ag.org.

CHAPTER ELEVEN

ACTIVELY SERVING

As the years of my life passed, I continued to ride the church bus, but now I was one of the teenage workers. Not impressed? I was. I remember the spiritual worth and pride I felt knowing that I was helping others. A group of us from the church went out on Saturdays to visit kids who had been missing from church services and to knock on doors and invite people to church. I remember knocking on one door and talking with a family who had a boy about my age. Soon he was riding the bus with me; eventually his entire whole family came to church and gave their lives to the Lord. I'll never forget the joy I felt, knowing that God had used me to reach this family for Christ. I didn't realize it at the time, but actively serving had become a cornerstone of my faith.

Each kid is searching for a place to belong, a place to discover their self-worth. Why not find it at church? Today thousands of young people flock to contests and events to put their talents to the test. Fortunately, churches seek to utilize these talents. Younger and younger teens are doing greater and greater feats of ministry by performing human videos, singing, playing instruments, giving sermons, and much more. These young people are using their talents in their churches. They are *actively serving* in ministry. This gives them a strong sense of self-worth and makes them feel valuable. It helps to cement their relationship with Christ through their daily activities.

As mentioned earlier Troy, Tonya, Trent, and Shane were part of a ministry team in our church so many years ago. At that time, I didn't realize how being involved in ministry was building fortitude into their spiritual foundations. It was clear to me that kids who had learned to seek God, hear His voice, follow His Word, and be led by the Spirit needed a place to minister. Ministry gives us the opportunity to seek God, prepare our lives, and lead others to Christ. For this group of young people it was children's ministry teams, doing ministry together to impact the lives of unsaved kids in our community. These four young people continued to live for God and to serve others their entire lives.

Earlier we quoted the four common factors mentioned by teens who had faithfully lived for God throughout their lives. Ministry was one of these key four elements. Teens who were involved in ministry said this gave them purpose as they continued to live for God.

Tips for Parents

Give your kids the opportunity to serve God in your community. Take them to an elderly person's home and together rake leaves, mow the lawn, or clean the yard. Give them the opportunity to feel their life is blessing others.

Give your kids the opportunity to minister at church. When they are *actively serving* it affirms their value to God and others. Let them see you minister on a regular basis.

Tips for Kids Ministry Leaders

Create opportunities for your class to minister to others. Teach your kids the value of hard work on behalf of someone else. Not only will you be depositing value in the life of each child, you will be helping to begin a good work ethic, which seems to be sorely missing in many young people today. Use kids' talents, interests, and skills. Use them as sound people, computer helpers, ushers, worship team leaders, and more. Look for ways to use them, and work with them to develop abilities to perform the tasks. You never know when God will speak to them about their future service to Him.

Affirm young people when they minister. For some of them, this is a huge step of faith. A kind word that they did a good job will give them confidence to continue in the future. God wants to use every kid. Each of them has God-given abilities He can use if you will encourage them and provide opportunities so they are *actively serving*.

CHAPTER TWELVE
BOLD IN FAITH

Dad was sort of a handyman. He learned it from his dad, my grandpa. For years, dad and grandpa were always building, remodeling, or changing something. My brothers and I became the work crew. Along the way I learned to do electrical work, plumbing, shingling, and carpentry. I learned to cut down a tree and install a toilet. I learned to do cement work and paint. No I'm not an expert, but somehow I gained the confidence and skills to get the job done. Now as an adult, I, too have remodeled some, built some, and fixed a lot. This wouldn't have happened if my dad and my grandpa had not given me an example to follow, a chance to learn, or an opportunity to succeed.

t's been said that a kid who leads others to Christ is less likely to walk away from Christ. If that's true, then it makes sense that being *bold in faith* is a strategic seventh goal for building enduring faith in kids' lives. Recall that when we discussed being *Spirit empowered*, we reiterated that one of the blessings of being baptized in the Holy Spirit is boldness to live for God and to serve Him. The disciples suddenly became bold in their faith after the Day of Pentecost. Peter, who was afraid to stand up for Christ, suddenly preached in front of thousands (Acts 2). Each of the disciples became bold men of God who worked fearlessly to spread the gospel.

So how do you help kids become *bold in faith*? The previous six goals are paramount for helping kids be bold. A kid who is powerful in prayer, is willing to pray on a moment's notice when they meet someone with

> **THE JOB OF KIDMIN LEADERS IS TO GIVE KIDS TOOLS TO HELP THEM BE BOLD IN FAITH.**

a need. A kid who has seen God do the miraculous, is a kid who will believe God for the miraculous once again. A kid who knows the promises found in God's Word, is more apt to share those promises with others. And a kid who knows the plan of salvation as written in God's Word, is more apt to have the courage to share that message with others.

I mentioned at the beginning of this chapter that I had learned to become a handyman. That happened because someone taught me. As I rode the bus to church and learned about God, I learned the tools to share my faith.

Winters in South Dakota are always cold. One way a young teenager can make money, if he doesn't mind hard work, is to shovel snow. I had several customers. One specific customer was an elderly lady. As I shoveled her walk one day I felt the Holy Spirit tell me that perhaps I was the only one who could tell her about Jesus. I didn't know her very well as I usually just spoke with her at the end of the day when I had finished shoveling her sidewalk. I remember praying for the opportunity to share the good news with her. I don't remember worrying about what to say because somewhere along the way, someone had instilled within me the plan of salvation and Scriptures that present the gospel. I was ready with the tools, and I was bold in the faith.

One day we got the storm of all storms. The snow was really deep! Wow! I shoveled snow first with a scoop shovel and then with a snow shovel. It was cold. I had finished about half the job when she called out the door and invited me up on the porch where she had two cups of hot chocolate waiting. I heard the Holy Spirit say, "This is the day you have been praying for." In those few moments as I told her the plan of salvation, a new soul found Jesus. Someday I will see her again in heaven. Not because I was so bold, but because faithful KidMin leaders had deposited tools within me that prepared me to obey God.

The job of KidMin leaders is to give kids tools to help them be bold in faith. Kids need to learn the plan of salvation through Scriptures and be able to share those verses either from memory or perhaps from a marked Bible. KidMin leaders can even play act with their kids—pretending to be an unsaved individual and letting the kids attempt to share the gospel.

A young girl named Mary had no intention of going to church. She hadn't been inside a church in years. But she loved going to parties. One bold young lady invited Mary to a party after a sports game. The party was at the teenager's house so Mary showed up. She was soon shocked to see a bunch of church kids at the party. She had a name for those kids: Jesus Freaks. Surprisingly, she soon found them to be nice. A friend at that party invited Mary to visit her church, and a few weeks later Mary found Jesus as her Savior. The boldness of one young lady is the reason my wife, Mary, and her entire family came to Christ.

The teenager who invited my wife to a Christian activity was prepared to be bold in her faith. Godly people had invested time and effort and love in her life, so she could bless others as she was faithful and bold.

Kids are naturally bold, but with a preparation and encouragement they become power-houses for God. They aren't afraid to pray for someone and believe God for a miracle. They aren't afraid to share the love of Jesus or invite someone to church. They aren't afraid to tell the stories of God they have heard. They want to be *bold in faith*. Let's give them a chance.

Tips for Parents
Share with your kids how you came to know Christ. Talk about people who helped you come to know Christ. Share with your kids the miracles God has done in your family. Encourage your kids to be bold in their faith. Encourage them to be ready when God gives them a moment to pray for someone with a need. Perhaps God will do a mighty miracle! Encourage your kids to learn Scriptures that explain the plan of salvation. Practice witnessing with your kids. Play act. Take turns pretending to be someone who doesn't know Jesus. Take turns being someone who needs help.

Tip for Kids Ministry Leaders

Share with your kids how you came to know Christ. Bring in other adults who have interesting testimonies of how their lives were impacted by others. Talk about the miraculous things God has done, especially when Christians acted boldly and believed God.

Encourage kids to watch for people who need prayer. Give them a chance to testify how God used them. Encourage kids to tell others about God's plan of salvation. Give them a chance to testify how God is using them. Encourage kids to invite people to church. Encourage kids to write letters to lost friends and loved ones inviting them to know Jesus.

Teach kids Scriptures that clearly articulate the plan of salvation. Allow time in class to for them to practice using these Scriptures to tell others about Jesus.

One great resource is ELIFE (Elife.ag.org). This free website offers materials designed to teach your kids to share their faith. It teaches kids to SEEK the Holy Spirit's guidance, to SHOW themselves friendly to others, to SHARE their stories of how God has helped them. Further it then instructs the kids to INVITE others to know Christ or to come to church, then to INVEST their lives in these new young believers.

CHAPTER THIRTEEN

LIVING LIKE CHRIST

King Josiah led the people of Israel in godly ways for many years. Through his repentance and godly influence hundreds of thousands or perhaps millions of people in the generations to come followed Jehovah. His father and grandfather were ungodly leaders, yet somehow because of unnamed teachers or leaders, he found God and lived a godly life (2 Kings 22). These unnamed individuals will reap amazing rewards for their faithfulness in reaching Josiah and helping him be obedient to God.

S tatistics show that the most effective opportunities for reaching and discipling individuals is while they are kids.[30] Parents have the best prospects for leading their kids in a powerful, purposeful faith in Christ. Yet many kids don't have Christian parents or they have parents who have abdicated this responsibility to the church. That's why the church must take action to ensure their kids receive not just facts about faith, but grow to develop a deep, true, and living relationship with God. Kids must discover God for themselves and learn to experience His presence regularly throughout their lives.

This book presents eight goals that together form a mighty spiritual foundation for kids. These goals are absolutely essential to building a spiritual faith deep into the bedrock of kid's lives. The eighth and final goal strives to help raise kids who are *living like Christ* now and for the rest of their lives. This goal is the culmination of the previous seven goals which include: *powerful in prayer, responsive in worship, biblically fluent, Spirit empowered, giving selflessly, actively serving,* and *bold in faith.* Each of these goals contributes to our ultimate goal of kids *living like Christ* for the rest of their lives!

Kids have a great capacity to learn. But if we don't teach them, they are at risk of falling astray. A great historical minister to kids—Charles Spurgeon notes,

> Children in grace have to grow, rising to greater capacity in knowing, being, doing, and feeling, and to greater power from God; therefore above all things they must be fed. They must be well fed or instructed, because they are in danger of having their cravings perversely satisfied with error.[31]

The eight goals in this book can positively impact the deep faith of children. Each lesson prayerfully prepared will impact the kids in your church.

When kids become *powerful in prayer*, their relationship with God grows deep because they know He is real. He has answered their prayers. Prayer brings kids into the presence of God where they discover Him, feel Him, sense Him, and watch Him answer their prayers. Through answered prayer they know He is alive.

As kids become *responsive in worship*, they fall in love with God. These kids have learned to progress from the outer courts of praise, where they merely sing about Him, into the inner courts, where they discover His close being. There they fall in love with their Creator and discover faith for a lifetime.

Kids who are *biblically fluent* have been introduced to God and His amazing Word. The Bible is a treasure for lifelong learning and obedience. Through Bible stories, kids learn the character of God. Through reading about the life of Jesus, they discover the love of God. And through God's promises, kids develop hope in God.

Spirit-empowered kids have discovered the amazing power of God and His willingness to involve Himself in their lives. They know the power of the Spirit to heal, answer, act, and work on their behalf. The

Spirit powerfully enables kids to stand their ground through the difficulties of life. This great gift provides power for service, boldness for witnessing, courage in times of difficulty, and assistance with prayer and praise.

Kids who are *giving selflessly* are kids who are passionate about the needs of the world. This is the heart of God. Every lost and needy person in the world is His child, loved by Him. God wants them to have the

THE SPIRIT POWERFULLY ENABLES KIDS TO STAND THEIR GROUND THROUGH THE DIFFICULTIES OF LIFE.

opportunity to know Him. Kids quickly grasp the loving heart of God and they develop a compassion that is hard to extinguish. This compassion anchors them to their deep faith as they endeavor to make a difference in the lives of others.

It's always a great joy to see kids who are *actively serving*. In service they put into practice their time, skills, and talents on behalf of others. When coupled with compassion, kids quickly desire to give back. They transition from being the one ministered to, to the one desiring to minister; from needing a Savior, to realizing the need of a Savior in others. Kids go from needing mentors, to being the one to mentor others. This goal builds young people who stand firm in their Christian faith.

Are your kids *bold in faith*? Do they have a passion to make a difference in people lives? Do they pray for lost relatives? Do they care about the sick? Do they share their faith? This goal clearly shows spiritual growth in the lives of your kids when they actively and boldly share their faith with others as they act the way they believe Christ would want them to.

Living like Christ—what a simple yet profound goal for each of your kids. Your desire should be that each of your kids would live for God the rest of their lives. When tested, they will stand strong. When scared, they will believe in God. When difficulties come, they will pray. When others are in need, they will help.

These eight goals complement every kids' church room and classroom. They provide the church with an intentional plan and blueprint for building a deep and lasting faith in kids. They provide the KidMin leader and parent with measurable goals for the spiritual foundation of kids.

Take a moment to study your kids. Look for intimacy with God when they are responsive in worship. Look for their powerful prayers. Encourage them to become Spirit empowered and biblically fluent. As they grow, encourage them to give selflessly, actively serve, and boldly live their lives like Christ!

As kids commune with God and He answers their prayers, this exposes the depth of their faith. When kids worship God, their closeness with Him becomes evident. Their comprehension of biblical values is discovered through the words they speak and the questions they ask. The ability to live like Christ is seen through their actions, their sacrifice, and their boldness. Step by step you can help to develop these eight goals in children.

Tips for Parents
Let these eight goals guide you as you build a deep and lasting foundation in your children. Teach them to pray, and let them hear you pray. Teach them to love God, and let them hear you express your love to God. Talk about the Bible. Let them ask questions. Search Scriptures together to see what God's Word says about different subjects. Talk with them about the gift of the Holy Spirit. Celebrate this gift that God has for them. Teach them about the lost and needy of the world. Encourage them to find ways to minister to those in need and minister at church using their talents to bless others.

Tips for Kids Ministry Leaders
Make these eight goals a priority in your ministry. Remember, finishing every aspect of the curriculum is less important than making God real to the kids and instilling a deep love for God in their hearts. It's so important that kids have the opportunity to discover God as their hero

through a personal relationship with Him, through prayer, and through worship. Make your classroom or kids' church a place where kids learn to pray and to love God.

Give kids the opportunity to ask questions about the lessons in the Bible. Involve them in the lessons—even allow them to take turns teaching various parts of the lesson. This really gives them the opportunity to study the Bible from a new perspective.

Introduce your kids to the gift of the Holy Spirit. Provide prayer time in class and in kids' church when your kids seem ready and have a desire to receive. Encourage them to also pray at home. Celebrate when kids are filled with the Holy Spirit.

Introduce kids to compassion, to ministry, and to sharing their faith boldly. Find ways to help them understand how lost people are, how needy they are, and how kids who love God can make a difference.

Kids who are *powerful in pray*er and *responsive in worship*, who are *biblically fluent* and *Spirit empowered*, will become spiritual champions. These kids have tremendous potential to live for God their entire lives. They will be *bold in their faith* as they *actively serve* the church. These kids will be *living like Christ* as they *give selflessly* all their lives.

A few years ago I found that forked tree on a campground that had been closed for a long time. I could no longer climb the tree, but I could remember what that humble place of prayer meant to me. Gratefulness and humility washed over me. I was grateful that God heard the prayers of a young boy; that He arranged for me to be discipled; and that He sent people to bring me to church on a bus each week. God raised up godly leaders to participate in giving me and my siblings a deep and lasting relationship with Him. I'm deeply humbled that so many people invested so much to help me.

Now it's *your* turn!

A LONGITUDINAL STUDY

FACTORS IN YOUTH AND YOUNG ADULT FAITH EXPERIENCE AND DEVELOPMENT[32]

1. Faith is deeply embedded in their family—their family identity and lifestyle.
2. At least three adult Christian mentors—coaches, employers, etc.—have played important roles in their lives.
3. They have engaged in three or more months of service in the name of Christ, as a volunteer missionary, camp counselor, etc.
4. They feel their church is "cool," which they define in terms of quality relationships, interesting preaching that tackles key questions, engaging music, worship, and a feeling that everyone is welcome and valued.
5. They feel they have been involved in some of the best ministry after Confirmation, in high school or college.
6. From the age of ten, their leadership has been invited by the church in many ways, such as playing the piano at events, etc.

ENDNOTES

1. George Barna, "Teenagers Embrace Religion but Are Not Excited About Christianity," *The Barna Update* Web site. Available from http://www.barn.org/FlexPage.aspx?Page=BarnaUpdate&Barna UpdateID=45. Accessed 11 November 2005, 3.

2. Ibid.

3. George Barna, "Teens Change Their Tune Regarding Self And Church," *The Barna Update* Web site; available from http://www.barna.org/FlexPage.aspx?Page+BarnaUpdate&BarnaUpd ateID+111; accessed 2 January 2006, 3. "There is evidence that spirituality has been mainstreamed into teen life without radically affecting the lifestyles and values of most teens."

4. Ibid., 6.

5. Ibid.

CHAPTER TWO

6. Ibid.

7. George Barna, *Transforming Children into Spiritual Champions* (Ventura, CA: Regal Books, 2003), 34.

8. George Barna, "Research Shows That Spiritual Maturity Process Should Start at a Young Age," *The Barna Update* Web site; available from http://www.barna.org/FlexPage.aspx?Page=BarnaUpdate& BarnaUpdateID=45; 26 November 2005, 1.

CHAPTER THREE

9. Randy Christensen, *Crucial Concepts in Kids Ministry* (Tulsa, Okla.: Insight Publishing, 2003), 18.

10. Scotty May, Beth Posterski, Catherine Stonehouse, and Linda Cannell, *Children Matter* (Grand Rapids, MI: Eerdmans, 2005), 71.

CHAPTER FOUR

11. Ibid.

12. C. H. Spurgeon, *Come Ye Children* (Pasadena, Tex.: Pilgrim Publications, n.d.), 84.

CHAPTER FIVE

13. Tedd Tripp, *Shepherding a Child's Heart* (Wapwallopen, PA: Shepherd Press, 2005), 90.

CHAPTER SIX

14. Dick Gruber, *Focus on Children* (Springfield, MO: Gospel Publishing House, 1993), 44.

CHAPTER SEVEN

15. "When someone is sitting alone in God's presence, adoring [worshipping] Him, speaking words of praise and thanksgiving to Him—this is the fruit of a genuine relationship with the Lord. It is the difference between doing something and knowing someone." Patrick Kavanaugh, *Raising Children to Adore God* (Grand Rapids: Chosen Books, 2003), 14.

16. Michael Card states, "What we have failed to recognize is that in all areas of ministry, it is simple, pure adoration [worship] that fuels our hearts and souls for God. The Bible comes to life only when we read it as a love letter from the One we adore." Quoted in Kavanaugh, *Raising Children to Adore God*. "Adoration is an intimate form of worship. It is about forming and nurturing an internal relationship with God." Ibid., 13.

17. James Dobson, *The Strong Willed Child* (Wheaton: Tyndale House, 1983), 21.

18. "Many children's services never move beyond a campfire sing-a-long. Week after week, children sing songs, yet rarely worship." Dick Gruber, *Children's Church: Turning Your Circus into a Service* (Springfield, MO: Gospel Publishing House, 1992), 33.

19. The authors describe means to give kids opportunities to write words of praise to God. Michael Clarensau and Clancy Hayes, *Give Them What They Want* (Springfield, M0.: Gospel Publishing House, 2002), 78.

20. Andy Park, *To Know You More* (Downers Grove, Ill.: InterVarsity Press, 2002), 49.

21. Randy tells of his own personal calling to the ministry as an eight-year old boy. Randy Christensen, *Crucial Concepts in Children's Ministry* (Tulsa: Insight Publishing, 2003), 45.

22. "Children who experience God's presence in worship and God's care through prayer will never be the same!" Tracy Carpenter, "*Same Old, NOT.*" Children's Ministry Magazine, May/June 2003, 53.

23. May, et al, *Children Matter*, 16.

24. Kavanaugh, *Raising Children to Adore God*, 155.

CHAPTER EIGHT

25. Sue Geiman, "The Key to Real Learning," *Children's Ministry Magazine* Web site. Available from http://cmmag.com/articles/detail.asp?ID=4961. Accessed 1 January 2006. 63.

26. George Barna, "Teenagers Embrace Religion but Are Not Excited About Christianity," *The Barna Update* Web site; available from http://www.barna.org/FlexPage.aspx?Page=BarnaUpdate&Barna UpdateID=45; accessed 1 January 2006, 2–3.

27. "A one-hour-a-week program will have difficulty providing children with all these essentials. Many churches offer several ministries for children—Sunday morning or evening learning hour, worship, clubs, and choirs—all of which can contribute elements to the curriculum." Scotty May, et al, *Children Matter*, 205.

28. George Barna, "Sunday School Is Changing in Under-the-Radar but in Significant Ways," *The Barna Update* Web site; available from http://www.barna.org/FlexPage.aspx?Page=BarnaUpdate&Barna UpdateID=192; accessed 1 January 2006, 2.

CHAPTER NINE

29. "Summer camp altars are filled with children responding to the gospel. Thousands are filled with the Holy Spirit each year." Christensen, *Crucial Concepts*, 23.

CHAPTER THIRTEEN

30. https://www.barna.com/research/evangelism-is-most-effective-among-kids/#

31. C. H. Spurgeon, *Come Ye Children* (Pasadena, Tex.: Pilgrim Publications, n.d.), 84.

APPENDIX

32. "Factors in Youth and Young Adult Faith Experience and Development: A Longitudinal Study," A Working Concept Paper, *Luther Seminary and Southwestern Seminary, Faith Factor* Web site; available from http://www.faithfactors.com/papers.htm; accessed 17 December 2005, 1.

FOR MORE INFORMATION ABOUT THIS AND OTHER
VALUABLE RESOURCES VISIT

WWW.MYHEALTHYCHURCH.COM

ABOUT THE AUTHOR

David Boyd served for eight years (1999-2007) as the National Children's Ministries Agency director for the General Council of the Assemblies of God and for eighteen years (1999 – 2017) as the National BGMC (Boys and Girls Missionary Challenge) director. Both he and his wife, Mary, have a tremendous vision for discipling kids, passing on the heritage of missions, and seeing the next generation grow into healthy adult disciples of Christ.

Prior to working at the national office, David and Mary served as full-time children's pastors for seventeen years. They led ministries with over 300 children's workers. Their final children's pastorate was at First Assembly in Fort Myers, Florida, under Dan Betzer. David is a graduate of North Central University, and holds an MA in theological studies from the Assemblies of God Theological Seminary.

David has written widely for Assemblies of God publications and curriculums. He is highly sought for national and worldwide children's conferences, camps, and seminars. He has a powerful ministry to deposit the depth of God's Word and the Spirit of God in the hearts and minds of kids and adult leaders. He has a desire to see kids taught in a way that helps them become believers who are "strong enough to last."